NATURALLY

Modern
Magick

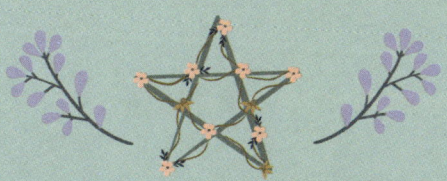

NATURALLY
Modern
Magick

The Essential Compendium
of Spells and Rituals for
Health, Happiness, and Prosperity

LACEY BURBAGE

Red Wheel

To the little witch in all of us:
may you always feel safe and free
to live your life openly.

This edition first published in 2025
by Red Wheel, an imprint of
Red Wheel/Weiser, LLC
With offices at:
65 Parker Street, Suite 7
Newburyport, MA 01950
www.redwheelweiser.com

ISBN: 978-1-59003-584-9

Library of Congress Cataloging-in-Publication Data available upon request.

Edited by Jennifer Calvert
Design by Melissa Gerber
Images used under license by *Shutterstock.com*.

Printed in China
WM
10 9 8 7 6 5 4 3 2 1

Acknowledgments

My sincere gratitude and love go to my husband and children. Thank you for being patient with me, even when I could not be patient with myself. Thank you for being part of a life that is too good to imagine, but that I had somehow always dreamed of.

I want to express my gratitude to my mom, my very first witchy role model. She shared with me her Tarot cards and incense, took me to watch *Practical Magic* at the movies, and never missed an opportunity to foretell if the fish were biting based on the cows in the pasture.

To my dad, who never hesitated to pass on his "aha!" moments, thank you. These conversations shaped my beliefs and inspired me to recognize the very real potential of magick.

To my brother, Donny: If I had to read this book to an audience, you would cheer the loudest and might even start a mosh pit. Thank you for letting me crash your shenanigans, for teaching me how to headbang, and for always being there.

Thank you to my Nana for imparting your wisdom and ways. You've connected me to a lineage full of traditions and fiercely independent women.

Mirth and reverence to the sages who have taught me the ways of their magick and craft. Merry meet and blessed be!

This wouldn't have been possible without my editor, Jen, who believed in me. Without either of us knowing it, writing this book healed my inner child. Thank you.

I'd like to express my gratitude to my online community for actively participating by asking questions and sharing their experiences. The content in this book draws inspiration from the genuine needs and desires that all humans share, yet it is us witches who understand how to use unique tools to turn our dreams into reality.

Finally, I thank the Goddess. For me to never know her would mean to never truly experience magick.

Introduction

The Limitless Magick of the Natural World

Do you long for a world where the limitless power of natural magick is at your fingertips? Where you can relax and let its gifts flow through you? I did once, too. As children, we have an innate bond with nature that works effortlessly. We instinctively wish upon dandelions, look to the clouds for shapes, and run barefoot in the grass. But, as adults, we can lose that sense of magick. *Naturally Modern Magick* can help you reconnect with it and create the life of your dreams.

Even as a longtime witch who had certainly used a plant or two in her practice, I felt lost in the hustle of a busy life. I wanted to feel more connected and in tune with the energies all around me—energies I had known since childhood but had grown disconnected from as more and more responsibilities took over. I had a thirst for that youthful feeling of curiosity and wonder. It wasn't long before I realized I wasn't alone. Rooted within each of us, there is an innate longing to embrace nature's wisdom and harness the magick of the natural world. We aren't waiting for it—it's waiting for us.

My own journey with natural magick began many moons ago, when I wandered into a tiny witchy shop on a historic Main Street. That day, I felt the call of the earth. As I gently pushed open the door, the aroma of incense caressed my senses, inviting me into a world of fascination. Shelves filled with apothecary jars lined the walls, dried plants hung from the ceiling like paper chandeliers, and scattered tables offered statues, beeswax candles, oil blends, crystals, and fresh herbs bundled and ready for a new home. I trailed my fingers over the items as I walked along, hungry to learn more about each and every one of them.

I moved to a back room filled with bookshelves and found an array of occult and herbalism books gracing their surfaces. After some time, and with a stack of books nestled in my arms, I made my way to the front register. At that moment, a plant I didn't know called to my spirit from amid the array of herbs. It felt like the earth whispered her name to me. Without hesitation, I found myself uttering, "And two ounces of damiana, please."

I walked as fast as I could to my car, the rustling of the autumn leaves urging me forward. I could sense divine essence in the intoxicating aroma emanating from the bag. In that moment, my entire life changed. I became completely infatuated with the healing power of plants and natural magick. Later that night, I would brew a tea of damiana and dedicate myself to learning the ways of green witchcraft.

As seekers of magick, we understand the inherent ability that resides within us all. It is a boundless potential for transformation and change that dwells within our spirit and yearns to be awakened. I created *Naturally Modern Magick* to help you activate and embrace yours.

Within these pages, you'll be guided by the wisdom of green witchcraft as it reveals the secrets of the healing and magickal powers of plants, animals, insects, and minerals. This knowledge comes from generations of people who have tended to their relationships with the natural world, earnestly learning about each element. With reverence, studying becomes an act of devotion, and tending to the land becomes a sacred offering.

You don't have to possess an extensive collection of herbs or be an expert gardener to access natural magick. I know I haven't always been fortunate in my own gardening endeavors. Despite having a humble witch's garden now, I still find myself killing even the most low-maintenance plants. But while others may look and see a yard full of dead plants, I choose to see a garden teeming with valuable lessons.

What I've come to realize is that the key to success in green witchcraft lies in connecting with the essence of natural elements and nurturing a meaningful relationship with them. It's not just about having a green thumb or an apothecary full of herbs, but understanding and respecting nature on a deeper level. This profound connection allows you to learn from your mistakes, appreciate the wisdom, and grow as both a witch and a person. Throughout this journey, you'll come to understand the cycle of rebirth and new beginnings that resides beneath the surface. In the quiet depths of the soil lies the potential for new life to sprout forth once again. Nature carries the gift of rejuvenation and growth.

Whether you are new to the craft or are a seasoned practitioner, it's not uncommon to feel overwhelmed or flooded with information when exploring the world of natural magick or to question whether you are doing it right. But, as you read, you'll discover a treasure trove of ready-made charms, spells, and rituals all meticulously crafted to amplify your connection with nature and to infuse your intentions with the divine energy of the earth. Immerse yourself in these spells and rituals, and they will become your spiritual companions, magnifying the power that already resides within you. That beautiful world of your childhood dreams, still brimming with green magick, will be yours.

The Basics of Natural Magick

Shortly after dedicating my studies to green witchcraft, I stumbled upon an overgrown garden tucked behind a barn at my grandmother's house. Seeing the lifeless plants resonated with me. I felt a sense of empathy for this forgotten space, which ignited a spark of inspiration within me. Determined to revive the garden, I began clearing the debris and nurturing the struggling plants. Nature became my teacher, offering lessons in resilience, adaptation, and the importance of harmony.

This is the key to natural magick: a strong bond with nature. By tapping into both your personal energy and the energy of the natural realm, you can interact and communicate with these energies, allowing you to manipulate them effectively. This is pivotal to achieving your desired outcome and can often be the difference between whether a spell succeeds or fails. With that in mind, here are a few things you'll need to understand as you work through this book.

The Nature of Energy

Magick is, in essence, a manipulation of energy, which is neither inherently good nor intrinsically evil. Instead, energy is a morally neutral power awaiting direction. Within the vast tapestry of interwoven threads that is the natural world, everything possesses a distinctive energetic signature, a unique vibrational essence that resonates within it. Through focused intention, you can shape and redirect that energy to achieve desired outcomes using symbolic actions and objects aligned with the energy.

Focused Intention

Concentrating on your intentions is crucial when practicing magick. While it's easy to identify our needs or desires, we often fail to consider the necessary steps to reach them or how we will feel once we have manifested them. This is where *focused intention* becomes essential. By directing your focus toward the emotions and sensations associated with receiving your desires, and reflecting on the steps it takes to get there, you align the mental, physical, and spiritual worlds to support your desired outcome. Communicating this hyper-focused intention to the ingredients you are using—especially those that align with your desired energetic vibrations—will amplify your magick.

Magickal Correspondence

Just like us, the natural world is multidimensional. Flora and fauna are complex and multi-faceted beings, possessing a plethora of physical, chemical, and *energetic* properties. Each of their distinct attributes has various associations depending on culture, tradition, and symbolism. Magickal correspondence is a long-held system linking natural ingredients, symbols, and gestures together energetically using the principles of sympathetic magick, or "like affects like." Understanding these magickal correspondences allows you to effectively communicate your focused intention when directing energy.

Hang around the cauldron with me long enough, and you're bound to hear me say, "I speak correspondences." That's because I've been working with them long enough that I've memorized how magickal elements link together. But even the most seasoned practitioners (myself included) need to reference a book every once in a while. You can find lists or tables of correspondences based on a variety of magickal traditions. When you look up any crystal or herb for its magickal properties, you'll find more than one intention and energy listed. For your convenience, I've included such a list in the Correspondences & Substitutions section (page 211) at the back of the book.

Magickal Tool versus Spiritual Kin

Your job as a wise witch is to develop a relationship and a means of communicating with your ingredients and elements. After all, if you'll be using them in your magickal work, you'll need to tell them what you want them to do. Developing a relationship with these natural elements is the difference between perceiving them as magickal tools and experiencing them as spiritual kin or partners. When you view plants and crystals solely as tools for your use, you tend to approach them with a transactional mindset, seeking to extract their benefits without considering their intrinsic value or interconnectedness. But, when you cultivate a deeper connection with your ingredients and recognize their inherent wisdom, they become more than just tools. They become spiritual supporters and collaborators.

This shift in perspective opens up a profound and mutually beneficial relationship. The simplest way to achieve it is to get to know the plants, crystals, and other ingredients that you use. Communicate your focused intention when working with them and feel their unique energy. Make note of how your energy works with each particular ingredient.

Initiating Spellwork

Before embarking on any magickal work, you've got to ensure that you are in the appropriate state of energy. This is vital to prevent miscommunication. It is not only your spiritual essence but also your physical and mental energy that matter. All three aspects must align harmoniously for successful results. A little prep work can go a long way toward getting you there.

Using Energetic Refreshers

We all need to take good care of ourselves when tapping into, manipulating, and directing various forms of energy. Otherwise, we leave ourselves vulnerable to energetic overload. Not only will this make your magick much less effective, but it can leave you feeling exhausted.

One of the best ways to both protect yourself and practice good spiritual hygiene is to do what I call an *energetic refresher* regularly. That means having various protective wards in place to ground and shield your energy, and to energetically cleanse yourself and your home regularly. In fact, I consider cleansing and protection magick so important that I dedicated Chapters 2 and 3 to it. Having an energetic refresher routine allows you to focus on your intention and the magickal work at hand. It can also act as a regular tune-up for your energy and help keep you grounded, even during mundane activities.

Beginning Magickal Workings

There are three main things I want you to do prior to performing any magickal work to ensure that you have what you need, you start off with a clean slate, and you can direct your energy toward the current magickal task. For the spells in this book, you should perform these three steps first:

- GATHER YOUR MATERIALS AND SET THEM OUT IN YOUR WORKING SPACE. Doing this beforehand ensures that you have all the necessary tools and ingredients readily available and within reach. I can't tell you how many times as a wee witch I forgot the matches or other important items after I started a ritual. These things are bound to happen. But, by setting up your working space first, you can avoid interruptions. You also establish a physical representation of your intention and prepare yourself for the upcoming ritual or spellwork. Not to mention, when you lay out all your items *before* cleansing, it makes it very simple and easy to cleanse everything in one fell swoop.

- **CLEANSE YOUR SPACE, YOURSELF, AND ALL ITEMS THAT YOU WILL BE USING.** This crucial step helps you remove any negative, stagnant, or otherwise unwanted energies that may interfere with your magickal work. There are many different methods of cleansing to help you reset the energy and create a fresh and sacred atmosphere for your practice. (You'll find a few in Chapter 2.) With that in mind, the spells and charms do not include separate instructions for cleansing, but remember to begin each magickal working by cleansing your materials, your workspace, and yourself.

- **GROUND AND CENTER YOUR ENERGY WITH MEDITATION.** These are two essential techniques for establishing a strong and stable energetic foundation, and they're covered in Chapter 1.

These fundamental steps help create an environment that is supportive of your magickal work by priming you for focused, uninterrupted channeling and directing of energy.

Casting a Circle

Some magickal traditions will call for casting a circle as an energetic boundary. You might do this for protection, to contain energy, or to separate the magickal work from mundane distractions. When and how to cast a circle is up to you. You may find it useful to cast a circle only for rituals or more elaborate spellwork. Use your intuition or rely on the guidance of your specific tradition. And if you're interested in casting a circle but not sure how to go about it, check out "Circle of Protection to Fortify Sacred Space" on page 45. I suggest casting a circle (if you choose to do so) after gathering all materials and cleansing yourself and the space but *before* grounding and centering your energy.

Using Incantations

An incantation is a form of communicating your focused intention to your ingredients and channeling and directing your personal power. The incantations within this book can be said out loud or to yourself—whichever feels right to you. Feel free to make changes to the wording whenever your spirit guides you to.

The Cardinal Directions

Some spells and rituals call for you to stand facing a specific direction (north, east, south, or west—sometimes called *cardinal directions*) and use a corresponding element as representation. These directions often align with the natural environment and the position of the sun in the sky. For those in the Northern Hemisphere:

- North corresponds to the element of earth, stability, and grounding.

- East corresponds to the element of air, new beginnings, creativity, and communication.

- South corresponds to the element of fire, passion, and energy.

- West corresponds to the element of water, emotions, and intuition.

For those in the Southern Hemisphere, you may need to adjust these correspondences to account for the opposite seasons, the location of the equator, and the natural flow of energy there. It is essential for practitioners to adapt their correspondences and rituals to their region and the natural world around them. Spend some time getting to know the landscape where you practice your magick and make adjustments to the cardinal directions and their corresponding elements that feel right to you and your tradition.

Divine Essence

Naturally Modern Magick is written in a nondogmatic and nondenominational manner. In green magick, we harness the powers of the earth to enhance our personal power. The magick lies in the connection between you, the ingredients, and their essence. Whether you work with animistic beliefs, deities, ancestors, or fae; simply connect with the essences of the earth and the Universe; or choose not to work with any spirits at all, you can incorporate these spells into your practice. You may also call in any being you wish to assist you with any of the charms, spells, or rituals in this book. However, the decision of when and how to do this, if at all, is entirely up to you and based on your personal practice. I've used "Universe" when writing some spells in this book. Feel free to swap or omit whatever feels right for you.

Understanding Consent

We're not only performing magick for ourselves. Oftentimes, we want to help friends and family, too. This is where we need to consider consent, which is important for ethical practice. It respects their autonomy—and boundaries—and aligns intentions while building a respectful relationship. So, if you want to help someone you care about, consider their wishes before doing magick for them.

Exercising Caution with Pets

When practicing witchcraft around pets, it's important to prioritize their safety and well-being. I grew up in a house full of fur babies, and I have a few familiars in my home today. Be cautious with burning candles and incense, as well as with toxic plants and essential oils. Keep crystals and altars out of their reach and create a separate space for rituals to prevent any disruption. Consider the energy you project and aim for a calm and positive atmosphere. Always prioritize your pets' comfort and consult with your vet if you are not sure what ingredients might be harmful to them.

Using Caution with Candles and Fire

Several of these spells use magickal techniques involving candles and fire. I typically call for using a chime candle, birthday candle, or rolled beeswax-sheet candle, as they dress easily and burn down fast. For any working that calls for a candle, you'll need matches and a secure candle holder. Magickally, it is best to let the candles burn down and extinguish themselves, but you can respectfully extinguish them with a candle snuffer. When anointing candles (see more on page 17), just be careful not to get the liquid on the wick (for fire safety).

Some workings call for burning paper or other items in a fireproof vessel. This can be a cast-iron cauldron, a cooking pot, or any container that is safe for this purpose. Be mindful of the surface you place the vessel on, as containers do get hot. And always follow these safety tips: hold the paper using tweezers or small tongs, keep a cup of water close by, ensure proper ventilation, and exercise caution when handling lit herbs or incense.

Dressing a Candle

A common technique that I use often with candle magick is dressing the candle, which can amplify your intention and enhance your spellwork. First, you use a sewing pin or other sharp object to carefully etch words or symbols into the candle. Then you anoint it with oil and roll it in a thin layer of dried herbs. You can even make your own candles (see "Spell Candles to Obtain What You Seek" on page 141).

Anointing Liquids in Magick

The special oils, potions, or other liquid substances that I refer to as "anointing liquids" are consecrated infusions with blessed magickal intention that you apply to objects, tools, or even yourself for empowerment. You can use any oil—even ones you already have at home, such as olive oil—as an anointing liquid. And you'll discover many spells within these pages where you can use it and enhance your magick. When anointing candles, just be careful not to get the liquid on the wick (for fire safety).

Crafting a Customized Sigil

Many workings call for a sigil, which is a design you create with specific magickal intent. The technique I favor for creating sigils involves using a triangle to represent creation. The base symbolizes a foundation or idea, and the two sides reaching upward symbolize actualization. You'll need a pen or pencil, paper, and a clear quartz point or a fireproof bowl.

First, spend a few moments focusing on your desired goal. Think of a simple word or phrase that embodies this goal and write it down. Cross out any duplicate letters and all vowels. For example, the phrase "attract love" would leave the letters "TRC" and "LV." Next, draw a triangle and write the alphabet inside the triangle, around the perimeter (see top illustration). Then draw a line that connects the remaining letters in your phrase in order (e.g., T-R-C-L-V). When you are done, you will have a basic design (see bottom illustration). Feel free to embellish this design with lines, dots, and any other marks that call to you until you're satisfied. Finally, activate it by either burning the paper over a fireproof vessel (using tweezers or tongs) or by tracing it on the paper with a quartz point, then drawing it in the air in front of you with your finger.

Personal-Tie Items

A personal-tie item is used in sympathetic spells to tether energies of a person to the magickal working. This can be a photo or drawing, a few strands of hair, a piece of jewelry, or another personal item. I regularly use personal-tie items in protection magick to safeguard myself or loved ones.

Disassembling a Spell

When a spell is complete, it's time to disassemble it. Each practitioner has their own unique approach to unraveling spells, so it's important to honor your intuition and tradition. Consider these factors:

- **DOES THE SPELL NO LONGER NEED YOUR ENERGY?** Disassemble it when the working is complete or no longer requires your input.

- **HAVE YOU EXPRESSED GRATITUDE?** Thank the energy and ingredients that assisted you, as well as yourself.

- **CAN ANY INGREDIENTS BE REUSED?** Cleanse and reuse items like charms, stones, and coins for eco-friendliness and cost-effectiveness.

- **IS IT SAFE TO COMPOST OR BURY?** Avoid composting nonbiodegradable materials and be cautious with plant matter to maintain ecosystem balance. I keep a container for used, dry, compostable herbs, which I regularly offer to the earth in gratitude to return their energy.

- **DOES IT NEED TO BE DISCARDED?** If repelling or banishing energy, dispose of nonreusable items in the trash. Reusable items can be cleansed for future use.

Cultivating a Future for Plants

As green witches, we understand that plants serve both our physical and spiritual well-being. They are our allies, teachers, and links to nature's energies. By preserving plant life, we honor our earth connection, maintain nature's balance, and ensure magickal ingredients for our rituals. Plant conservation and sustainability let us give back to our nurturing earth and preserve sacred traditions for generations. Please be mindful of your impact and support organizations like United Plant Savers, dedicated to protecting plants at risk from overharvesting and habitat loss.

"The Universe is
full of magickal
things patiently
waiting for our
wits to grow
sharper."

—EDEN PHILLPOTTS

Chapter 1

Grounding & Centering

Have you ever just felt "off," like your energy is cluttered? Or are you finding it hard to focus? You may need to ground or center yourself. Your personal energy serves as the foundation for all your magickal endeavors, so you want to ensure that it's at its best. Grounding plays a vital role in promoting stability and achieving a balanced state of mind. It's also helpful after performing magickal work so you won't take all that raised energy around with you all day, as it could be disruptive. Centering yourself before spellwork aids in aligning your thoughts and emotions, bringing them into a harmonious state and enhancing your ability to focus, concentrate, visualize, and effectively manifest your intentions. Both types of rituals, grounding and centering, are essential to your practice.

SIMPLE GROUNDING MEDITATION

Let's face it: we're modern witches with modern lives. We don't always have the time to sit in meditation for hours. You can create a solid energy base with this quick grounding meditation, which is great to use for magickal work or anytime you need to stabilize your spirit. The connection it allows you to forge ensures that you remain rooted and balanced, guarding against any potential imbalances or overwhelming energy accumulation.

⇝ Instructions ⇜

1. Find a quiet and comfortable space. Close your eyes and take a few deep breaths, allowing yourself to relax and let go of any tension.

2. Visualize yourself standing in a beautiful forest.

3. Imagine that roots are growing from the soles of your feet deep into the earth. See these roots extending with strength and stability, reaching down into the rich soil below.

4. As you connect with the earth, feel its energy flowing up through your roots and entering your body. Visualize this energy as a warm and grounding light, slowly rising through your legs, up into your torso, and spreading throughout your entire being.

5. Release any accumulated energy that no longer serves your well-being by allowing it to flow down your roots and be neutralized by the earth. Simultaneously, feel yourself absorbing positive energy from your surroundings.

6. As the earth's energy fills you, imagine it bringing with it a sense of stability, strength, and balance. Allow this energy to anchor you, grounding you firmly to the earth and providing a solid foundation for your spellwork.

Create Your Own Guided Meditations

To enhance your experience with meditations, I recommend recording yourself reading them aloud. This way, you can listen to the recordings later as guided meditations. Feel free to adapt or modify any meditation to suit your preferences and intentions.

ENERGY-BALANCING ELEMENTAL GROUNDING MEDITATION

Sometimes you need a little more help harmonizing your energy. Maybe you're doing an elaborate ritual with more detailed intentions, or maybe you need to bring your personal energy back to a state of balance. Either way, this elemental grounding meditation is designed to give your grounding work a boost. Consider this meditation your spiritual spa day.

⇶ Instructions ⇷

1. Find a comfortable position, either sitting or lying down. Close your eyes and take a few deep breaths, allowing yourself to relax and let go of any tension.

2. Notice the sensation of each inhale and exhale, allowing your breath to become slow, deep, and steady.

3. Visualize yourself standing in a serene and beautiful forest by a flowing river. Feel the solid ground beneath your feet, connecting you to the element of earth.

4. Imagine roots extending from the soles of your feet, anchoring you deep into the earth's core. Feel the stability, strength, and grounding that the earth provides.

5. Now bring your attention to the gentle breeze that flows through the air around you. Feel the coolness and lightness of it caress your skin, connecting you to the element of air.

6. As you continue to breathe deeply, take in the freshness and scents of the natural world around you and imagine that you are drawing in the revitalizing energy of the air. Visualize this energy entering your body with each inhale, bringing clarity, inspiration, and freedom.

7. Next, visualize the vibrant sun shining brightly above you, its rays reaching your skin and filling you with a deep warmth that permeates to your core. Imagine the sun transforming into a vibrant and dancing flame in the sky, symbolizing the element of fire.

8. As you bask in the sun's radiant energy, feel the intense warmth, passion, and transformative power it embodies. Embrace the energy of the sun's fire as it fuels your intentions and guides you toward your goals.

9. Now turn your attention to the flowing river beside you, symbolizing the element of water. Feel the gentle movement and fluidity of the water. Allow its cleansing and purifying energy to wash away any negativity or stagnant emotions within you.

10. Notice how the water effortlessly adapts to its surroundings, flowing and shaping itself to fit any container or terrain. Draw inspiration from its adaptable nature, recognizing your own capacity to navigate life's challenges with grace and flexibility.

11. Embrace the qualities of each element within you.

12. Now imagine a radiant light in the center of your being, representing your essence. Feel this light expanding and radiating outward, connecting you to the divine and the infinite.

13. Allow the energy of the Universe to balance all the elements within you, blending them into unity. Feel the harmony and interconnectedness of all these elements within your being.

14. Take a few moments to embrace these feelings of strength, clarity, inspiration, and connection.

15. When you're ready, gently bring your awareness back to the physical space around you. Wiggle your fingers, wiggle your toes, take a few deep breaths, and gently open your eyes. Slowly allow yourself to return to the present moment, carrying the grounding and centering energy of all the elements and the Universe with you.

ROOTED TRANQUILITY SPELL

This grounding spell will stabilize your personal energy so that you can feel rooted and secure in your magick. Valerian's unique energy and aroma brings an extra-special grounding quality to the working, infusing it with calmness and serenity and reminding you to slow down and find peace within. You'll put the charm in your shoe overnight to ensure that you carry this stable energy with you on your journey.

Materials

Dried valerian root

Brown candle

Anointing oil

Hematite crystal

Small pouch

Pair of your shoes

Instructions

1. Sprinkle some valerian root onto your work surface. Dress the brown candle with your name, starting at the top and moving toward the base, then anoint it with oil in the same direction before rolling it in the valerian root.

2. Light the candle. As the flame flickers, visualize any chaotic or scattered energy within you being drawn toward the candle's flame. See it leaving you and, as it does, feel yourself becoming more centered and grounded.

3. Hold the hematite crystal in your hand. Feel its cool, grounding energy as you close your eyes. Let its energy flow through you, anchoring you to the earth's energy.

4. Add some valerian root to the pouch, then top it with the hematite crystal, allowing the two energies to blend and charge each other.

5. Place the pouch with the valerian root and hematite inside your shoe while saying:
   "With each step I take, I am rooted and stable.
   With each step I take, I am grounded and secure."

6. Leave the shoe to charge overnight. In the morning, remove the valerian root from your shoe and sprinkle it outside the door you use to enter and exit your home. Carry the hematite with you or sleep with it under your pillow.

MUSHROOM EARTH SPELL BOTTLE FOR GROUNDING PERSONAL ENERGY

The summer I moved into my first apartment was a whirlwind of excitement and anxiety. Packing, moving, and setting up a home for the first time in a tiny little space made me feel like I had a truly never-ending to-do list. One day, it was just too much for me to take. When I eventually pulled myself off the floor, I grabbed my witch's journal to jot down this spell. It brought me a great deal of comfort and stability, and it can help you, too. Just be sure that all your ingredients are completely dry—especially the mushrooms and dirt—lest you end up with a moldy spell bottle.

Materials

Brown candle or sealing wax

Small, corked glass bottle

Dry dirt or soil from outside

Black tourmaline, hematite, obsidian, red jasper, or smoky quartz stones

Dried mushrooms of any kind

Spanish moss, carpet moss, or reindeer moss

⇝⇝ *Instructions* ⇜⇜⇜

1. Light the brown candle or begin melting the sealing wax. Uncork the small bottle, place it on your working surface, and add some of the dirt or soil. Concentrate your focused intention on achieving a state of energetic balance and grounding as you fill the vessel.

2. Next, add the crystals that you've chosen. As you do this, concentrate your focused intention on bringing stability into your life.

3. As you add the dried mushrooms, consider what type of growth you want to come from this magickal working.

4. Finally, add the dried moss to the bottle and bring your attention to how you want to stay rooted within yourself.

5. Once all the ingredients are in the bottle, replace the cork, hold it to your heart, and say:

    "My roots are deep, I stand firm and strong,

    in harmony with nature, where I belong.

    As above, so below, as within, so without,

    grounded and balanced, there is no doubt.

    The power of the earth and me,

    I am forever grounded in my energy."

6. Drip the candle wax or sealing wax over the top of the bottle, sealing your intention and the cork in place. You can carry this bottle with you daily, but it's especially helpful to hold in stressful situations and during meditation.

EARTH'S EMBRACE OIL BLEND FOR IMPORTANT DECISIONS

This grounding blend of essential oils is one of my favorite scents in the world. Its earthy smell evokes memories of a shop my mom and I used to visit—a combination of metaphysical shop, bookstore, and organic deli all in one. After moving away, I spent years trying to recapture that mineral-rich essence that cradled you the moment you walked in the door. This is it. In this spell, hematite brings strength and stability, while vetiver, cypress, and smoky quartz aid in balancing and grounding. Mugwort, often associated with witchcraft, is used for enhancing psychic abilities and intuition while patchouli is grounding. Use this blend any time you need more insight or have an important decision to make.

Materials

2-ounce dropper bottle

Carrier oil, such as grapeseed

Cypress, mugwort, patchouli, and vetiver essential oils

Small brown or green candle

Hematite and smoky quartz stones

1. Fill the dropper bottle with the carrier oil, leaving a little room at the top.

2. Next, add 2 drops each of the essential oils. Replace the top and focus on anchoring your energy to the earth. Then shake your intention into the bottle.

3. Apply a few drops of the oil mixture to the top of the candle, avoiding the wick. Gently spread the oil toward the base and yourself.

4. Light the candle. As it flickers, envision the warm and nurturing energy of the earth embracing you. Take a few deep breaths to center yourself. Feel the connection between your body and the ground beneath you.

5. Next, anoint each of the crystals with a drop of the oil. As you do this, say:

   "Resting deep within the earth's embrace,

   I ground my energy and find my place.

   With clarity and wisdom, I now can see,

   which path is the right one for me."

6. Place the hematite and smoky quartz near the candle, allowing them to absorb the energy of the flame.

7. Sit in quiet meditation for a few moments. This is also a good time to do divination regarding the situation. The spell's grounded energy may help you find clarity.

8. Allow the candle to burn out, if possible, or respectfully extinguish it and relight it consecutively with the same intention until it is finished.

Carry the Energy with You

Keep the hematite and smoky quartz with you as grounding talismans, refreshing them with a drop of oil when needed. You can also use the oil to anoint yourself, a deck of Tarot cards, or another form of divination when you find that you need to ground your energy.

Simple Everyday Grounding Charms

Incorporating simple grounding charms into your daily life can help you maintain your personal energy by keeping you centered and balanced. Here are some examples:

- Try a 1-minute visualization where you envision yourself as a rooted tree, drawing energy from the earth through your deep-reaching roots.

- Spend 2 minutes "earthing" by connecting directly with the earth's energy through bare feet or hands outdoors. Alternatively, practice a walking meditation, paying attention to each step and the sensations underfoot.

- Carry or meditate with grounding crystals like hematite, smoky quartz, and black tourmaline.

- Keep grounding herbs such as horehound, mugwort, patchouli, and vetiver with you in a pouch.

- In the morning, light a brown or green candle, focusing on its flame as you set your intention to ground your energy for the day.

- Trace and stir sigils designed for grounding into your morning coffee or meal.

- Recite grounding mantras or chants that resonate with you.

- Take a ritual bath filled with earthy herbs or salts that correspond with cleansing and grounding.

- Spend time near trees to access their rooted energy.

- And finally, the simplest—yet not the easiest—practice of all: just breathe. Breathwork will help you anchor yourself in the present moment.

SIMPLE MEDITATION TO CENTER YOUR ENERGY

You don't have to look very far in any witchcraft or magickal community to learn that intention is an important aspect of your magick. Centering your energy means giving your complete focus to your intention to strengthen your spellwork. I know—it's easier said than done. That's where this simple but powerful meditation comes in handy.

⇒ Instructions ⇐

1. Take a moment to find a comfortable position where you can close your eyes.

2. Take three deep breaths. With each breath out, visualize feelings, thoughts, and emotions that don't align with your intention moving outward and away from you. Feel them exit your body as the warm air rushes out. On the last breath, exhale loudly.

3. Inhale again, visualizing or stating your intention in your mind. Feel the cool, refreshing air rushing in and revitalizing every part of your being.

4. Breathe in deeply a few more times, inhaling all the energy that supports your goals.

5. On your last exhale, blow the renewed energy out and into your working space.

UNIVERSAL CENTERING MEDITATION FOR AMPLIFYING INTENTION

This meditation ritual is designed to harness the vast collective energy of the Universe and channel it toward focused concentration. Use it when you want to amplify your intention or pursue particularly ambitious magickal goals.

⟫⟫ Instructions ⟪⟪

1. Find a place where you can sit or lie down comfortably—a place where you will not be disturbed and where you can close your eyes.

2. Begin by taking a few deep breaths. As you breathe, start counting backward from ten.

3. With each breath, begin to relax more and more: ten . . . becoming relaxed . . . nine . . . more relaxed . . . eight . . . even deeper into relaxation, and so on. When you reach one, you are completely and totally in a state of relaxation, ready to receive energy from the Universe.

4. Visualize yourself sitting on top of a hill or mountain at night, with the stars all around you. Everything is surrounded by darkness, and all you can clearly see are the shimmering lights that dot the sky. Feel the cool, damp night on your skin and hear the sounds of crickets chirping nearby.

5. As you completely immerse yourself in this landscape, golden light begins to flow from above into the crown of your head. This light fills your body with radiant energy flowing through your entire being. It is here to support you on your journey.

6. Once your body is completely filled with the radiant, glowing light, you notice your hands beginning to tingle. When you look down, you see tiny sparks of golden light coming from your fingers. These tiny sparks allow anything you touch within your working to be imbued with your intention and Universal energy that connects you to the infinite divine essence.

7. With each breath you take, the light grows brighter and brighter until you can no longer see anything but white because of its brilliant glow.

8. Spend as long as you need letting this light charge you and your intention.

9. When you are ready, see the blinding white light slowly grow smaller until it is once again golden and contained within you.

10. Take another deep breath and begin counting backward again from ten. This time, with each number, you slowly bring your awareness back to the present moment. Ten . . . wiggling your fingers . . . nine . . . wiggling your toes, and so on until you are completely in the present moment and filled with the energy needed to give your full attention to your work.

Chapter 2

Cleansing

Cleansing is something I prioritize in my own practice. These rituals are commonly performed at either the beginning or the end of a cycle, such as when you move to a new home, introduce something new into your life, finish something, or even just prepare for spellwork. In this section, you will find charms, spells, and rituals that are designed to cleanse, purify, and create a balanced sanctuary of positive vibrations for you and your spellwork.

JUNIPER SMOKE CLEANSING FOR MENTAL CLARITY

When I joined my first coven, we would gather together to make incense, often using the juniper that grew alongside one of the members' homes. Making a central ingredient used in our rituals became a beautiful reflection of our community. Through these rituals, I formed a special bond with this plant and many of the women who became my mentors.

Juniper is highly regarded for its purifying properties and is known to promote mental clarity while grounding and centering. One of the ways it can offer these benefits is through smoke cleansing, which restores positive energy while dispelling negative or stagnant energy. Use this cleansing ritual at the beginning of any magickal work or whenever you need an energetic tune-up.

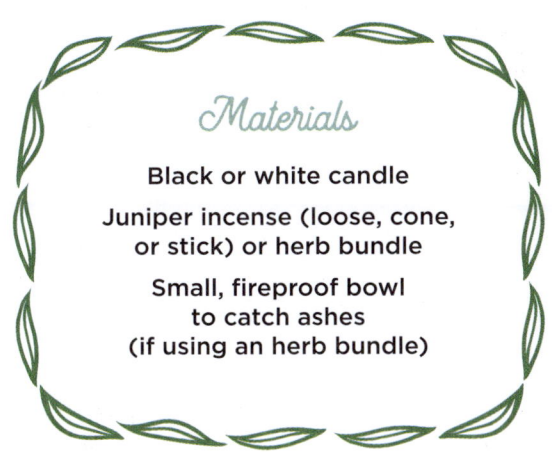

Materials

Black or white candle

Juniper incense (loose, cone, or stick) or herb bundle

Small, fireproof bowl to catch ashes (if using an herb bundle)

➤➤ *Instructions* ◀◀

1. Stand in the center of your working space and light the black or white candle.

2. Focus your intention on what it is that you want to cleanse.

3. Spend a few moments concentrating on retuning the present energy.

4. When you feel ready, safely light the end of the juniper incense or herb bundle from the flame of the candle. Let it take as much time as it needs to fully catch, then allow any flame to smolder.

5. Once the incense or herb bundle is smoldering, and you can see a steady stream of smoke, visualize the smoke as a gentle waterfall cascading down, refreshing and revitalizing everything it touches.

6. Start by first cleansing yourself. Bring the incense or herb bundle near your feet and, in a motion that feels right to you, slowly move it up the front of your body to the top of your head.

7. Hold the smoke above your head for a few moments and visualize it flowing down your back, all the way to the floor, cleansing every part of your physical and spiritual being.

8. Next, you can cleanse any object that you like by passing it through the smoke. Or, if you would like to cleanse a space in preparation for a spell or ritual, move about the working area in a counterclockwise direction, enabling the smoke to clarify the space.

Cultural Respect

Smoke cleansing has been utilized for centuries in diverse cultures and spiritual traditions. It involves burning plants or incense and using the smoke to cleanse a person, space, or object. When engaging in smoke cleansing, it is crucial to approach the practice with respect, mindfulness, and intention. It's also worth further research to better understand the various cultural and traditional contexts surrounding this type of cleansing and the plants used.

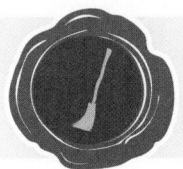

Simple Broom Charms for Cleansing and Protecting Your Home

You'd be hard-pressed to find a symbol as synonymous with witches as the broom. Also known as a besom, the broom holds symbolic and magickal significance in various traditions and practices. It has widely been associated with witches dating back to the Middle Ages.

In witchcraft, the broom is a tool for sweeping and clearing sacred spaces. This can be symbolic, where the bristles do not physically touch the floor, or practical, where they may come into contact with the ground. Both approaches are valid and acceptable. Sweeping from east to west invites energies, while sweeping from west to east banishes energies. Clockwise sweeping invites, and counterclockwise sweeping casts out.

Sweeping with a broom symbolizes clearing away negative energy and preparing for sacred or magickal work. It also represents transitions, signifying the removal of the old to make way for new beginnings. Because it is made from natural materials, the broom is often linked to the element of earth and its grounding properties.

There are many ways to incorporate brooms into your practice: Hanging a broom over the front door offers protection by keeping negative energy out and positive energy in. You can keep a broom near every door or window of your home. When something negative occurs, pick up the broom and sweep the energy out while bidding it goodbye. When life feels chaotic, you can sweep the outside entryway to help bring balance. When you feel stuck in life, you can sweep stagnant energy out of the corners of your home. And finally, you can place a broom under the bed to aid in dream work and astral projection while providing protection from psychic attacks. Just remember these tips when cleansing with brooms:

- Placing a broom outside during a thunderstorm is said to charge it with potent energy.

- You can ask house spirits to assist in cleansing by joining you in sweeping.

- Avoid sweeping at night, which can disturb weary souls.

- And never bring an old broom to a new home—you don't want to bring in old energy and "dirty" up the new place!

MULTIPURPOSE MOONLIGHT CLEANSING & BLESSING ESSENCE

The first time I ever made this multipurpose cleansing spray, I felt like I had discovered a hidden treasure. Charging water with the essence of the full moon imbues it with the moon's purifying and protective energy. And it can be used in so many ways. One of my favorites is to freeze it to use as ice cubes to make any drink a little more magickal. You can also spray yourself with it when you want to cleanse and protect your energy field, or sprinkle it over new water-safe tools to cleanse and ready them for magickal work.

The only materials you truly need to make moon water are water and a jar—everything else is simply an added boost for focusing and communicating your intention. By using lunar colors, crystals, and herbs, you can amplify your connection to your goal. You can also use a vessel to hold the water while it charges. This can be as simple or as fancy as you like, but I suggest choosing one that calls to you and dedicating it to making charged water.

Materials

Vessel (optional)

Jar or bottle for storage

Spring or purified water

Salt (optional)

White, blue, gray, or silver cloth

White, blue, or silver tray or plate

Moonstone, selenite, jasmine, rosemary,
or any other herbs or crystals that correspond
with the moon or purification and protection

⇶ Instructions ⇜

1. During a full moon, fill your vessel or jar with water. If you are using purified water, add a tiny bit of salt so its vitality will be reawakened by the minerals.

2. Lay a cloth out on the ground or on a surface outside, ideally in an area that will be shaded first thing in the morning. If you cannot set up outside, try utilizing a window where the moon's presence is still easily felt.

3. Place the tray or plate in the center of the cloth. Then place the water in the center of the tray.

4. Add the crystals and herbs in a circle around the water in any arrangement that feels right to you.

5. Hold your hands to the sky for a time, absorbing the energy from the full moon and allowing it to completely wash over you.

6. Hold your hands over your heart and visualize the moon's energy filling your heart with an illuminating glow.

7. Next, hold your hands over the water and say:

    "I call upon the moon's presence,

    to imbue this water with your essence.

    With energy pure and bright,

    charge, protect, and cleanse with your lunar light."

8. Let this magickal working sit out for at least an hour, preferably overnight. Then transfer your moon water to the bottle or jar, if you used a vessel, and seal it. The moon water will remain effective for up to 1 month when stored in the refrigerator.

What If Sunlight Touches My Moon Water?

This is a hotly debated topic in the witchcraft community. Personally, I believe that the water is not tainted even if the sun touches it. We are very specific in communicating our intention when calling upon the moon and asking for its essence to assist us. It's also worth considering that the moon is always present—even during the day—and is illuminated by the sun's light reflecting upon it. But, ultimately, you need to do what resonates with you and aligns with your beliefs.

Magick-Enhancing, Moon-Water Cleansing Spray

Water is a force to be reckoned with! It is an incredibly potent cleansing element, possessing both destructive and replenishing properties within its steadily flowing powers. Whenever you're in need of quick cleansing and protection, place clear quartz in a small spray bottle and fill it with moon water. If you don't have moon water available, you can add non-magickal water, moonstone, and clear quartz to the spray bottle. Then simply spray yourself, your space, and any water-safe tools as needed.

When you infuse water with the essence of the moon, you gain the additional support of the moon's magickal properties: enhancing intuition, soothing emotions, purifying and cleansing energy, and amplifying magickal intentions. Enlisting the assistance of clear quartz for clarity and spiritual connection further amplifies your magick. Adding another dimension to this simple charm by incorporating a moonstone brings heightened intuition, protection, and dream work.

Crystal-Clear Salt and Charcoal Cleansing for Rooms and Objects

Salt is a valuable tool for every witch, as it creates a barrier against negativity, clears and purifies spaces or objects, and has a reputation for healing. This practical charm combines salt with charcoal, which absorbs negative energy, and a clear quartz point, which amplifies energies and spiritual connection. For even more magickal oomph, perform it on a Monday (the day of the week associated with the moon) to draw on the moon's emotional healing and cleansing properties.

On a Monday night, set up a bowl containing salt and charcoal with a clear quartz point positioned upward in the center. If you want to cleanse a room, place the bowl in the center of the desired room. To cleanse an object, place the object on top of the mixture, beside the quartz point. For personal cleansing, put the bowl under your bed. Let the bowl remain intact overnight or for a few days. Once you feel the cleansing is complete, remove the bowl, dispose of the salt and charcoal in the trash, take the trash outside, and wash the quartz under running water.

SIMPLE SOUND CLEANSING TO REBALANCE VIBRATIONS

When you require a quick but thorough energy revitalization and harmonization, sound is a powerful tool. Its inherent vibrational qualities can actively engage with the energies in a given space, effectively disrupting stagnant or negative energies. That's why there's such a rich history of sound being used in cleansing and purifying rituals in cultures and belief systems around the world. Besides, sound has the added benefit of relaxing and uplifting the mind, body, and spirit. This ritual embraces sound's power by using just a bell, chime, drum, tambourine, rattle, or any other instrument you like. I've even known people to bang pots and pans together, so don't be afraid to get creative!

Materials

Your instrument of choice

Instructions

1. Begin the process of cleansing yourself by allowing the vibrations to wash over you as you play the instrument with a rhythmic and deliberate pace. Take your time, ensuring that each ring or sound fully envelops you. Take as many long, deep, cleansing breaths as you need. You'll know your energy is revitalizing when you begin to feel calmer and more centered.

2. To achieve harmonization of your environment, move in a clockwise spiral around the room, beginning in the center and expanding outward. Maintain your rhythm of sound as you move, ensuring a continuous flow until you reach the walls.

3. Do this in every room of the house once per season or after having houseguests, big parties, or other events. And do it more frequently in any room with a lot of energetic activity, such as the living room or any room where you regularly practice magick.

SPELL TO SEE IF SOMEONE HAS SENT MALICE YOUR WAY

How do you know when you need to cleanse? While it never hurts, this ritual can help you uncover whether potential hexes, curses, harmful intentions, or negative energy have been directed toward you. In this method of divination—known as cleromancy, sortilege, or casting—the reader tosses or casts small objects and then interprets the resulting arrangement to gain insight. Casting cinnamon sticks adds psychic-enhancing properties, protection, and cleansing. You can use anything to divide the space, such as simply placing a book in the center. However, I find a little painter's tape most useful. After you're finished, you'll simmer the cinnamon sticks you cast to remove any negative energy that might be lingering.

Materials

3 cinnamon sticks of the same size

Masking tape

Tongs or broom and dustpan

Pot of water

Salt

->>>> *Instructions* <<<<-

1. Find an area where you have plenty of room. Use the tape to make a dividing line in the middle of the floor, designating one side of the space for yes and one side for no.

2. Position yourself around 5 feet away from the mark, with the mark behind you.

3. Holding the cinnamon sticks in your right hand, deeply inhale their aroma, envisioning it cleansing you from within.

4. Now move the cinnamon sticks over your entire body in a back-and-forth or "S" motion, visualizing the cinnamon sticks absorbing any negative energy. Start from the top of your head, slowly pass over the front of your body and move down to your feet, then move up the back of your body. As you do this, say:

   "Ill intent upon me, is it true?

   Yes or no, cinnamon, what say you?

   Reveal the answer, oh spicy bark of the tree,

   and cleanse away any malice sent to me!"

   Then toss the cinnamon sticks as straight as you can behind you.

5. Turn around to see how they fell. The side with more cinnamon sticks (yes or no) will reveal your answer.

6. Use tongs or a broom and dustpan to pick up the cinnamon sticks and put them in the pot of water without touching them.

7. Place the pot on the stove, add a pinch of salt, and let it simmer as long as you feel necessary, adding water as needed.

8. When you are done, use the tongs to pull the cinnamon sticks out of the water and throw them in the trash. Sprinkle another pinch of salt over the trash and pour any remaining water down the drain.

A HEX-BREAKING RITUAL TO REMOVE NEGATIVE ENERGY

The beauty of natural magick is utilizing the magick in everyday things, like fruit and ice. In this ritual, lemon or lime serves to dissolve negativity and cleanse away malevolent influences, while angelica root acts as a ward against negative energies. Fruit pits are particularly effective in breaking hexes due to the protective outer shell they possess, representing a natural defense mechanism against harmful influences. And the ice represents immobilizing negativity and halting its expansion. Perform this ritual at night during the waning moon to enhance its banishing energy and the efficiency of this magickal working.

Materials

Black candle

Vessel

Water

Salt

Lemon or lime juice

Ground angelica root

Ice cubes

Pit from a stone fruit, such as a peach, apricot, nectarine, or cherry

Fresh sprigs of rosemary

⤞ Instructions ⤝

1. Place your vessel in the center of your working space. Light the candle, hold it, turn to the east, and say:

   "By the power of flame, I invoke this rite."

2. Turn to the south and say:

   "To banish negativity and restore my light."

3. Turn to the west and say:

   "Sacred flames, burn away all ill."

4. Turn to the north and say:

   "Let negativity dissolve, according to my will."

5. Pour the water into the vessel, paying close attention to the sound it makes. Let its rushing and splashing serenade you with cleansing energy.

6. Add the salt, lemon or lime juice, angelica root, ice cubes, and fruit pit to the water. Then stir the mixture in three counterclockwise circles followed by an "X" across the center of the vessel.

7. Visualize the ice pushing ill intent away from you. Feel the icy barrier obstruct negativity, preventing its expansion.

8. Carefully drip some wax from the candle into the mixture.

9. Dip the rosemary into the mixture, then use it to sprinkle water onto yourself. Then sprinkle the mixture within your home, along your walkway, around your entryway, inside your car, or any place where you regularly spend time, such as an office. Place any leftover mixture, along with the rosemary sprigs, on your bedside table overnight.

10. In the morning, remove the fruit pit. Keep it with you as a protective ward. Hang the sprigs of rosemary over your front door or bed, or continue to keep them on your bedside table until the next waning moon. Then scoop out the wax, throw it out, and flush the remaining mixture down the toilet.

Chapter 3

Protection

Energetic protection forms an essential layer of defense in any solid witchcraft practice. In this chapter, you'll practice the essential art of fortifying your personal energy, warding against unwanted influences, and safeguarding your loved ones. Warding can prevent future impacts, whereas protection spells and rituals can help shield you against any negative forces currently directed your way. You might perform these when you think you've been affected by the evil eye, experience a streak of bad luck, or sense an underlying unease.

CIRCLE OF PROTECTION TO FORTIFY SACRED SPACE

The circle isn't just your average geometric shape—it's like a magickal force field. Appearing everywhere from ancient architecture to nature, this powerful shape is also more than a boundary. Within its curves, energies harmonize, intentions amplify, and the mundane yields to the magickal.

Casting a circle during a ritual allows you to build your very own spiritual temple. I prefer to reserve it for workings beyond everyday spells or charms, weaving it into rituals that beckon the manipulation and channeling of energies within consecrated spaces. You can perform this circle casting before any ritual in this book, but it would particularly benefit the Earthen Amulet against the Envious (page 53), Alchemical Lunar Ritual for Shadow Work (page 85), Blessing Ritual for Starting a New Job or Career Path (page 109), and Blessings Abound Gratitude Ritual (page 129). If you don't have a wand or other tool for directing energy, simply use your finger.

Materials

Salt

Cup or bowl of water

Fresh or dried thyme

Fresh rosemary sprigs
or bundle of sage (optional)

Wand, athame, ritual sword,
or staff (optional)

⇝⇝⇝ *Instructions* ⇜⇜⇜

1. Stir the salt into the water clockwise using your finger, invoking blessings and fortification.

2. Stir the thyme into the water clockwise using your finger, invoking strength.

3. Place your hands over the mixture to bless it by saying:

   "Blessed be this water, pure and true.

   All is cleansed, balanced, and renewed."

4. Gather the rosemary or sage into a small bouquet, then dip it into the water and use it to sprinkle the water around the perimeter of your sacred space in a clockwise direction while saying:

   "A haven of safety, a sanctuary of might,

   I call upon magick to guard this sacred site."

   Alternatively, you can use your fingers instead of an herb bouquet to sprinkle the water.

5. Repeat step 4 a total of three times.

6. Next, use your finger, wand, athame, ritual sword, or staff to symbolically draw a clockwise circle around the perimeter of your space.

7. Visualize a circle of blue light radiating around you. See it, immaculate and unbroken, enfolding you in its protective embrace.

8. Raise your hands up and see the light transforming into a dome that stretches over you. Smooth your hands around this dome, shaping, fortifying, and molding its protective energy around you.

9. Move your hands down and visualize the blue light expanding below you, into the earth, and forming a protective sphere all around you.

10. Once you feel completely shielded and safeguarded, perform your ritual or other magickal work.

11. After you've performed your ritual, close the circle. This can be done by walking the perimeter again and symbolically erasing the circle with the bouquet of herbs or your finger, athame, ritual sword, or staff in a counterclockwise direction while saying:

    "The circle is released, expanding this magick of mine,

    open, yet unbroken, for all time."

A POPPET FOR PROTECTION

A poppet is a doll that serves as a symbolic representation of an individual's energy, and it can be a useful tool for protecting yourself and loved ones. You can make a simple poppet for use in any spell from paper or cloth or even by gluing a photo onto a pouch. But incorporating tourmaline and salt, which absorb negative energy, with rue, which dispels malevolent intent, gives this protection poppet its power. This spell's effects are particularly heightened if you perform it during a full moon, when you can invoke its protective prowess. You can also call upon Artemis (goddess of the moon), the Universe, or any other being to whom you feel connected.

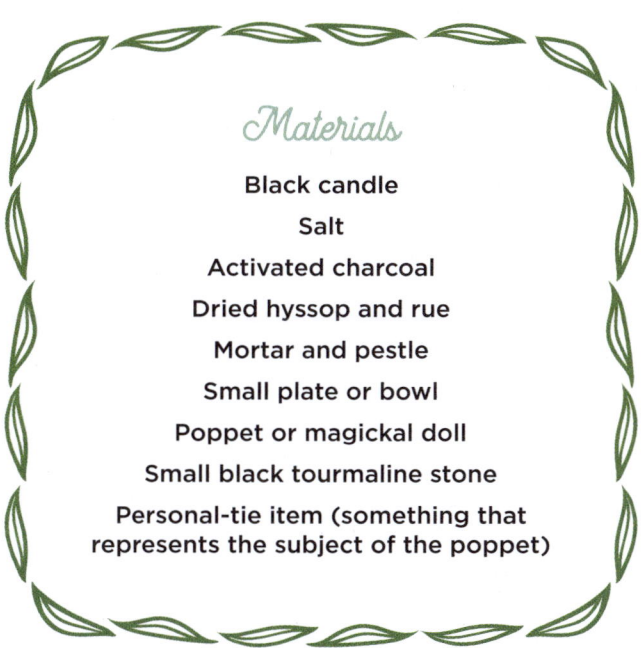

Materials

Black candle

Salt

Activated charcoal

Dried hyssop and rue

Mortar and pestle

Small plate or bowl

Poppet or magickal doll

Small black tourmaline stone

Personal-tie item (something that represents the subject of the poppet)

⤜⤜ Instructions ⤛⤛

1. Raise your hands to the sky and say:

    "I call upon the healing and protective energies of the Universe.
    May you guide me on my path and shield me from harm."

2. Then light the candle and say:

    "Candle black as night,

    remove this inner blight.

    Absorb any and all negative energy,

    so that I may restore my vibrancy."

3. Add the salt, activated charcoal, hyssop, and rue to the mortar. Grind them until well incorporated.

4. Sprinkle a small amount of the salt mixture onto the plate (or into the bowl) and place the poppet on top. Focus on your intention and, once you feel ready, stuff the black tourmaline and personal-tie item into the belly of the poppet.

5. Place the poppet back onto the salt and envision a vibrant, radiant light flowing through it, representing the protective being you called on for assistance. Then say:

    "May your powers amplify and harmonize,

    providing me with strength, vitality, and defense."

6. Take a moment to focus on your intention for health and protection. Visualize yourself or your subject surrounded by a glowing energy shield, impenetrable by illness or negativity.

7. Express gratitude for the protection you seek, then allow the candle to safely burn out.

8. Place the poppet with the plate or bowl of salt under your bed. Charge and cleanse it regularly.

BOTANICAL GUARDIAN TO WARD AGAINST HARM

There's something so invigorating about wandering through rows of lush greenery, envisioning a vibrant garden taking shape. Folklore suggests that optimism may be a product of the plants themselves. It also tells us that some plants perish because they have absorbed the negative energy and ill intentions of a hex or curse. This spell uses a houseplant to harness the protective potential of plants. To anyone else, the plant you choose will seem like just another potted friend. But it will serve you as a guardian of your energetic harmony. For added protection, you can use the Raven Ward Multi-Use Protective Salt (page 51) as well as the Botanical Shielding Oil (page 57) or Multipurpose Moonlight Cleansing & Blessing Essence (page 36).

Materials

Salt

Potted plant

Black candle

Anointing liquid

Pen and small piece of paper

Crushed dried eggshells

Small cup or bowl of water

Dried marjoram

Smoky quartz stone

⇁⇾ Instructions ⇽↼

1. On a large working surface, sprinkle the salt counterclockwise to create a circle big enough to surround your plant. Place your plant in the middle of the circle.

2. Anoint the black candle with the liquid, moving from the base of the candle up and away from you and being careful to avoid the wick.

3. Sprinkle a small amount of salt on your surface and roll the black candle in it. Set the candle back in its holder and light it.

4. Use the pen to draw a protective sigil or symbol on the paper and fold it away from you.

5. Bury the paper in the plant's soil, then sprinkle the crushed eggshells on top of the soil.

6. Place the cup or bowl of water in front of you and add the marjoram to the water.

7. Put your hands over the water and imbue it with your intention and essence, tethering it to you.

8. Wash your hands in the water mixture while saying:

   "Guard this place from harm and ill,

   through realms unseen, this is my will."

9. Pour the water over the soil of your plant, then place the smoky quartz in the soil and move the plant to its new home.

Caring for Your Guardian

Choose a plant that is easy to care for and that you know will thrive where you place it, and make sure you pay close attention to it and care for it on a regular schedule. If you do this but notice that the plant is in distress, you'll know that someone may have sent malice your way. Help the plant protect you by performing the cleansing spell of your choice.

RAVEN WARD MULTI-USE PROTECTIVE SALT

Salt is protective on its own, but there's always room for improvement in magick. This spell combines elements known for protection, purification, and the repulsion of unfavorable energies to create a potent black salt that acts as an energetic shield. Botanicals like sage, rosemary, and hyssop safeguard against harmful influences. Activated charcoal (easily found in capsule form at health-food stores) or ashes (made from burning protective herbs or incense) absorb negativity while also lending the salt its black appearance. Eggshells and onyx add an extra layer of defense, making this black salt the perfect ingredient for almost any spell or ritual that calls for salt's protective qualities.

Materials

Jar with lid or cork

Sea salt or rock salt

Mortar and pestle or electric coffee grinder

Activated charcoal or ashes

Dried angelica, hyssop, mullein, rosemary, and sage

Crushed dried eggshells

Any combination of basil, black pepper, cedarwood, juniper, lavender, patchouli, rosemary, and sage essential oils

Onyx stone

~>>> *Instructions* <<<~

1. Add the salt to the mortar or electric coffee grinder, then grind it while thinking about cleansing and banishing negativity and unwanted energies.

2. Add the remaining ingredients (except the onyx stone) one at a time, grinding each into the other and invoking protection.

3. Once the black salt mixture is well combined and completely charged with protective magick, transfer it to the jar.

4. Place the onyx inside the jar and seal it, or seal the jar and place the stone on top. Either way, always store them together.

Charms and Uses for Black Salt

You can utilize the power of black salt in various ways to enhance protection and cleansing:

- Sprinkle it along the inside perimeter of your home to create a shield against negative energies.

- If your salt contains skin-safe ingredients, enhance your personal energy by adding a pinch of black salt to your bathwater.

- Elevate your candle magick by anointing candles and rolling them in black salt (especially helpful in banishing rituals).

- To create a protective amulet, gather black salt in a small pouch and carry it with you.

- Consecrate your sacred space by sprinkling black salt around it while infusing it with purifying energies.

- Incorporate black salt into your protective or banishing sigils.

Any way you use it, black salt will reinforce your intentions with its potent energy.

EARTHEN AMULET
AGAINST THE ENVIOUS

One of the most powerful ways to practice protection magick is to wear or carry with you something that has been charged with that intention. This is an all-purpose amulet in that you can wear it as jewelry, hang it over a doorway or a rearview mirror, keep it at your desk, or carry it in your purse or pocket. It can also be helpful in warding against the evil eye. Blackberry leaf will shield you, rue will protect you, and marigold will safeguard you against harm, bad luck, and deception. You can make it out of any type of clay that you like to work with, but I really enjoy natural clays like terra-cotta. If you want to kick things up a notch, add some color magick by mixing pigments into the clay or painting it after it dries.

Materials

Dried blackberry leaf, marigold, and rue

Crushed dried eggshells

Mortar and pestle

Clay

Small eye hook (optional)

⇢⇢⇢ *Instructions* ⇠⇠⇠

1. Add the blackberry leaf, marigold, rue, and crushed eggshells to the mortar and grind them into a coarse powder. As you do this, envision a protective shield all around you.

2. Knead the herb mixture into the clay while envisioning an energetic fortification against negative energy and saying:

   "I ward away any and all bad luck,

   ill will, and envy that comes my way."

3. Mold the clay into any shape that feels protective to you, such as an eye, a spiral, or a heart. You may also carve or imprint a design into the clay.

4. Insert the eye hook into the top of the amulet or poke a small hole through the clay so that you can insert a cord or chain into it later.

5. Let the clay set and harden per the manufacturer's instructions.

6. After the clay has fully hardened, hold it in your hands and say:

   "I am cloaked in a shield of protection."

7. Charge and cleanse your amulet regularly.

The Evil Eye

The "evil eye" has historical and cross-cultural significance rooted in the belief that a malevolent gaze can bring harm, misfortune, or curses upon individuals. This concept has been carried through the ages across the world. In some of the many cultures that observe it, the evil eye is known as *nazar*, *malocchio*, and *drishti*. Because its power is often attributed to jealousy, envy, or malicious intent, there's a long-held custom of crafting amulets (like this one) to mitigate its negative effects.

BITTERNESS TO BLESSINGS SPELL TO TRANSMUTE BAD ENERGY TO GOOD

A simple egg is a powerful symbol. Not only does it have a barrier of protection, it also harbors the profound potential for transformation and rebirth. This spell combines cleansing and energy-transmuting herbs with an egg to transform negative energy into positive energy. Decorating the exterior of the egg with symbols and sigils that represent blessings helps enhance the energy flow all around you. That decoration can be as straightforward as using a permanent marker to draw protective runes and symbols, or as intricate as covering it in pressed flowers.

Materials

1 fresh egg

Sewing pin or small nail

Gray candle or sealing wax

Decorations of choice

Pen and small piece of paper

Dried rosemary and sage

Cedar and juniper essential oils

Personal-tie item or strand of hair

Instructions

1. Use the sewing pin or nail to poke a small hole, about the size of a lentil, in each end of the egg. Wipe the hole on the rounder (bottom) side of the egg clean with soap and water or a disinfectant wipe, then press your lips to it and gently blow the contents of the raw egg into the trash (or into a bowl to save in the fridge for later).

2. Thoroughly, but gently, rinse the eggshell by running water inside it, carefully shaking it up as you plug the holes with your fingers, and emptying it out. As you do this, envision the water not only physically cleansing the egg but energetically preparing it for your magick.

3. Light the candle or heat the sealing wax and seal the bottom end of the egg, leaving the top hole open.

4. Once the wax has cooled and the bottom of the egg is sealed, you can proceed to decorate the egg with elements that symbolize blessings and protection. Use your name to create a sigil with the intention to transform any negative energy or ill intentions directed toward you into prosperity, good luck, opportunities, or anything else you'd like. Design it in such a way that whenever someone speaks your name or thinks of you, the energy transforms into blessings that come your way. And write it on the small piece of paper.

5. Roll the paper as small and tightly as you can, so that it will slip into the hole you made at the top of the egg.

6. Add your personal-tie item or strand of hair to the inside of the egg, then add a sprinkling of the herbs and a few drops of each essential oil.

7. Leave the top of the egg open to allow energy to flow into the charm, and leave the egg on your altar, on your desk, under your bed, or on a shelf that you pass by often.

8. Charge and cleanse the egg under moonlight or with crystals such as selenite regularly.

Customize It

Look in the Correspondences & Substitutions section on page 211 for other herbs that support your intentions, and add those to your egg. For example, you might add cinnamon for abundance or clover for luck.

BOTANICAL SHIELDING OIL

Incorporating magickal oil blends into spells is one of my favorite ways to practice natural magick. Just as each plant carries its unique energetic signature, the oils derived from them also possess distinctive qualities. Crafting blends can involve infusing plants into a carrier oil, mixing essential oils with a carrier oil, or combining both methods. (Note: If you want to keep any plant material in an oil bottle, use dried plants to avoid mold.) This oil blends protective essences with clear quartz and black tourmaline to harmonize energies and magnify intentions while also creating a shield of energy around the wearer. Use it whenever you feel you need a little extra energetic security.

Materials

2- or 4-ounce dropper bottle

Black tourmaline and clear quartz crystal chips

Dried chrysanthemum

Olive or castor oil (or other carrier oil)

Any combination of black pepper, cedarwood, cypress, eucalyptus, juniper, lavender, rosemary, and sage essential oils

Instructions

1. Add the crystal chips to the bottle, followed by a pinch of dried chrysanthemum.

2. Fill the dropper bottle with the oil, leaving a little space at the top.

3. Add 12 drops total of your preferred essential oils to the bottle. As you add each drop, focus on the feeling of having a shield of protection around you.

4. Close the lid to your dropper bottle and shake in your intention.

5. Hold the bottle in the palms of your hands and bring them to your forehead while envisioning a protective energy all around you.

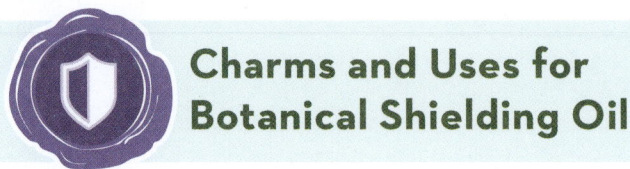

Charms and Uses for Botanical Shielding Oil

For those seeking to harness this oil's protective energies, here are some magickal uses and charms:

- Anoint your living space by applying it to doorways and windowsills, forming a barrier against negative influences.

- Infuse your amulets and talismans with its power to create personal shields.

- Establish an aura shield by sweeping a few drops over your body, reinforcing your energetic boundaries.

- Enhance your intuition practices by anointing your third eye before divination, creating a shield against disruptive energies.

- Utilize it for cleansing rituals, anointing candles for focused spellwork.

- Create dream protection by anointing sachets under your pillow.

- Inscribe protective symbols on candles anointed with the oil for a formidable barrier spell.

- Carry it to ensure safety during travels.

- Use it on your body and in your hair to fortify your energy in stressful situations.

- Anoint a blue lace agate, clear quartz, hematite, emerald, or jasper stone with it on a Wednesday, then carry it with you to protect your peace.

Through these methods, the oil becomes a versatile tool to infuse life's many facets, both seen and unseen, with protective energies.

WARD WEAVER WITCHES' LADDER OF PROTECTION

Witches' ladders are ropes or cords with knots or braids used to weave a magickal intention. By combining knot magick and color magick, they fortify and seal protective barriers, amplifying your magickal strength. As you create your magickal working, you'll say a word or incantation that resonates with your intention for each knot. You can also incorporate trinkets or charms that have protective or special significance to you, such as beads, bells, crystals, feathers, flowers, keys, or seashells. Your ladder doesn't have to look a certain way or contain a specific number of knots—the design is up to you. And you can craft it for yourself or for a friend as long as you utilize the hair of the person you wish to protect. When you're finished, you'll hang your ladder of protection by the primary entrance of your home, in your car, or at work.

Materials

3 strands of sturdy, black cord, 1–2 feet long

3 strands of hair

Personal-tie items (optional)

✎✎✎ Instructions ✶✶✶

1. Secure your focused intuition in your mind. Imagine that you are weaving a safeguard for yourself or your loved ones.

2. Gather all three strands of cord and the hair, tie them together in a knot about 2 inches from the top, and say:

   "Guarding."

3. Tie a knot in one of the combined strands while adding one of your trinkets, if you choose to use them, and say:

   "Shielding."

4. Continue tying knots, adding trinkets as you go, each time saying a different protective word, such as:

   "Warding."

   "Safeguarding."

   "Defending."

   "Repelling."

5. Once you're happy with your creation, hang your protective charm. Be sure to charge and cleanse it regularly.

Before You Gather Natural Treasures

It's important to be mindful if you choose to collect feathers and other objects from nature. Many places have laws that safeguard wildlife and their homes. It's wise to get to know the local laws and guidelines to protect yourself and the local ecosystem.

SPELL TO SAFEGUARD A FRIEND

Practicing a combination of candle and color magick is a simple and easy way to offer magickal protection for a friend. A black candle can expel negative energy, whereas gray is useful for neutralizing it. Black pepper and agate come to your friend's aid for added protection. And mint stands ready to lend a hand by cleansing and purifying any harm that may come their way.

Materials

Sewing pin or other sharp object for etching

Black or gray candle

Ground or whole black peppercorns

Fresh or dried mint

Agate stone

Instructions

1. Dress the candle with the person's name, starting at the top of the candle.

2. Sprinkle the peppercorns and mint in a circle around the candle.

3. Place the agate next to the candle inside the circle.

4. Light the candle and allow it to burn all the way down while you visualize a forcefield of protection encasing your friend.

5. When you're finished, gift your friend the charged agate to carry.

SAFE-TRAVEL PROTECTION SPELL

Travel protection is an age-old concept. In ancient Rome, soldiers commonly wore medals adorned with images aimed at harnessing apotropaic powers. Across the globe, people still wear diverse amulets and pendants believed to provide protection for safe travel. Be it for your daily commute or an upcoming adventure, this charm is brimming with herbs and crystals that ensure secure journeys. You can wear it like a Roman, hang it from a rearview mirror, or wrap it around a hotel doorknob or luggage handle.

Materials

Multipurpose Moonlight Cleansing & Blessing Essence (page 36) or stick incense

Necklace pendant jar, small jar, or pouch

Salt

Dried angelica, basil, mullein, and rosemary

Black tourmaline stone

Pen and small piece of paper

Black candle or sealing wax

Black cord

1. Cleanse the jar inside and out using the cleansing essence or incense, and allow it to dry, if need be.

2. To the jar or pouch, add the salt, herbs, and black tourmaline while focusing on protection and safety.

3. Write the rune Algiz/Elhaz (ᛉ) or another protective symbol or sigil on the paper and kiss it three times.

4. Light the black candle or melt the sealing wax and drip some wax over the rune on the paper.

5. After the wax has cooled and hardened on the paper, roll the paper and place it in the jar or pouch.

6. If using a jar, cork it and drip wax over the top and sides, focusing on sealing everything inside.

7. Tie the black cord around the neck of the bottle, thread it through an eye hook, or tie it around the pouch so that your charm can be worn or hung.

Cunning Ways to Elevate Protection

Make your personal style about more than mere aesthetics and take it into the realm of magick by weaving protection into your jewelry and hair accessories, making them conduits of safeguarding energy. When you bring home a new accessory, cleanse your new magickal ally with the Crystal-Clear Salt and Charcoal Cleansing for Rooms and Objects spell (page 38) or your preferred method. Then consecrate your accessories by blessing them, imbuing them with your intention, and anointing them with protective oils. For a magickal boost, consider selecting items that are already adorned with protective gemstones or symbolic charms. Keep in mind that regular cleansing and charging under the full moon are vital to maximize this magick and help sustain its vigor. And for a more profound connection, go beyond jewelry and consider enchanting your hair by weaving into it a protective braid. As you intertwine your hair with your magick, you tie in your intention for shielding and protection.

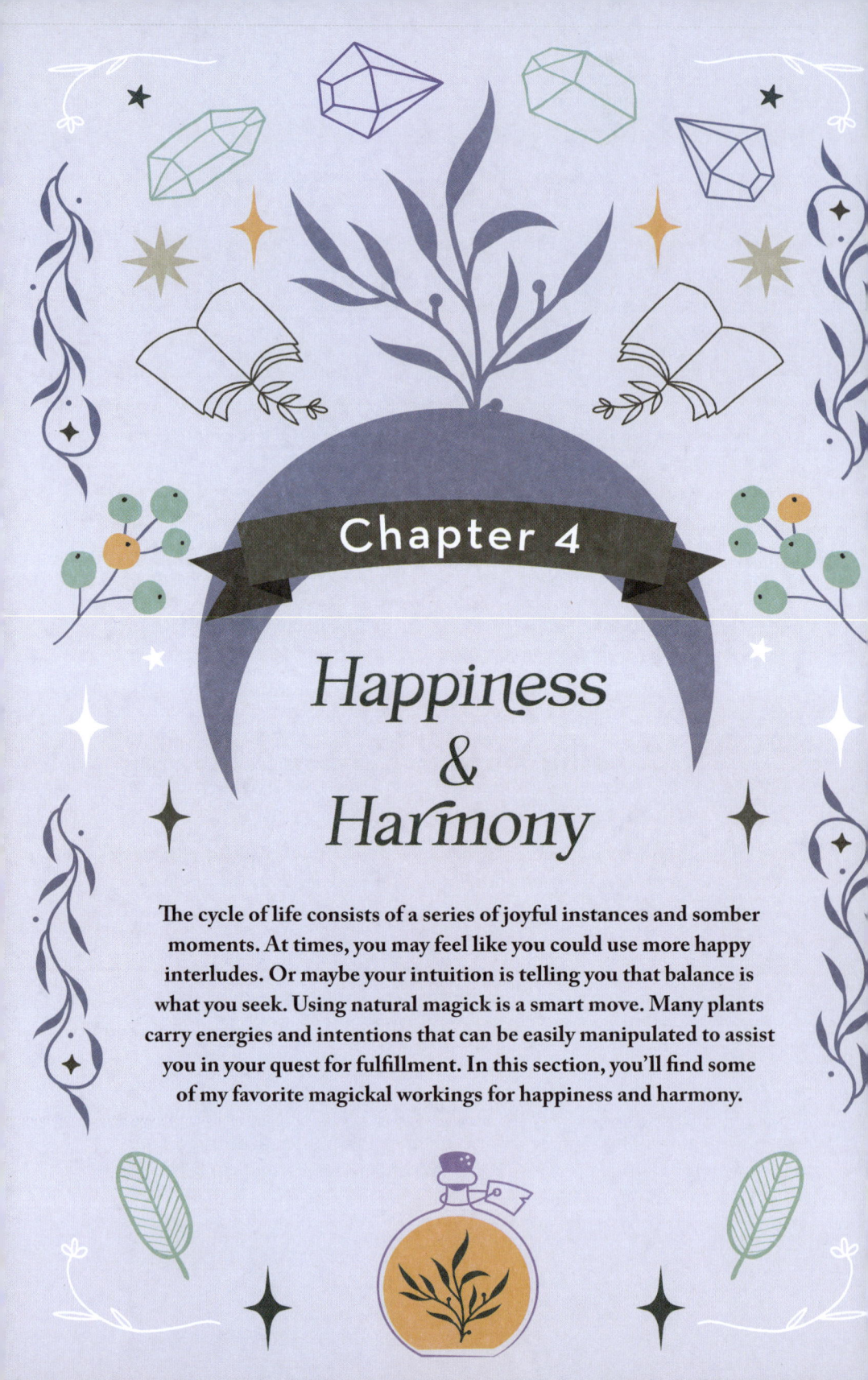

Chapter 4

Happiness & Harmony

The cycle of life consists of a series of joyful instances and somber moments. At times, you may feel like you could use more happy interludes. Or maybe your intuition is telling you that balance is what you seek. Using natural magick is a smart move. Many plants carry energies and intentions that can be easily manipulated to assist you in your quest for fulfillment. In this section, you'll find some of my favorite magickal workings for happiness and harmony.

SPELL BOTTLE TO BRING HAPPINESS & WELL-BEING

Spell bottles are especially helpful for inner work because they can address the feelings and emotions we keep bottled up. In this working, you'll utilize the symbolism of the bottle to represent any suppressed feelings and address them with color magick in the form of a yellow candle, which represents happiness and clarity. Incorporating an aster, a flower that embodies true happiness on every level, will brighten your life. This cheerful spell also uses saffron to invoke healing and joy, rose for love, lavender for peace, yarrow for communication, sage for granting wishes, and honey for sweet rewards. I like to use corked test tubes for my spell bottles—they are quite pretty on display and are small enough to carry. However, any container with a lid will work.

Materials

Yellow candle

Bottle or jar with lid

Fresh or dried aster, lavender, rose petals, saffron, sage, and yarrow

Honey

⇒≫ *Instructions* ≪⇐

1. Light the candle and set it safely to the side.

2. Add the ingredients to the bottle or jar one at a time. As you do this, say:

   "Where I go, happiness follows.

   There is no more room for any sorrows.

   I am authentic, whole, and complete.

   Everything that I am makes life sweet."

3. Place the top on your bottle or jar and use the candle to drip wax over it to seal. Let it dry.

4. Keep the spell bottle in your home or carry it with you to infuse your day with happiness.

Charm to Release Worries

Another method to relieve stress and worry is to speak your concerns into a glass of water before pouring it down the drain. Avoid looking at the water as you do this so that you don't reabsorb the energies. Then sprinkle a little salt over the drain to ensure that all your stress is cleansed away. This practice aims to give physical shape to your worries, making it easier to let go. Harnessing the element of water and pouring it out symbolizes releasing, cleansing, and moving on from those concerns.

SERENITY SOAK FOR RELAXATION & A CLEAR MIND

Make a truly comforting spell by blending herbs known for bringing about serenity with crystals that vibrate love, healing, and balance. This calming bath ritual calls for amethyst, clear quartz, and rose quartz to create a soothing bath experience. If you are unable to take a bath, use it as a foot soak instead. This soothing mixture can be made in advance and used over and over again. For even greater relaxation, combine it with Tranquilitea (page 69) and Calming Essence Relaxation Incense Blend (page 78).

Materials

Sea salt

Dried chamomile, lavender, passionflower, rose petals, and rosemary

Amethyst, clear quartz, and rose quartz stones

Sachet or cloth tea bag

1. In a mixing bowl, combine the sea salt, chamomile, lavender, passionflower, rose petals, and rosemary.

2. Stir the mixture clockwise to invoke relaxation, clarity, self-love, and self-empowerment.

3. Use a utensil or your finger to draw an infinity symbol (a horizontal figure eight) into the mixture. Then add about ¼ cup of the mixture to the sachet.

4. Draw a warm bath and place the clear quartz, amethyst, and rose quartz into the bathtub so that they are submerged in bathwater and arranged in a triangle shape, pointing toward you.

5. Add the sachet to the water and let it steep in the bath as you soak.

6. Relax into the water and take a few deep breaths, or even meditate if it is safe to do so, focusing on the calmness of the moment.

Crystal Considerations

There are a few things you'll want to consider before using crystals in a bath. First, make sure your crystals are water safe. Amethyst, clear quartz, and rose quartz all have a mineral hardness of 5 or greater on the Mohs Hardness Scale, which means water won't damage them. Next, clean your crystals before adding them to the water because there are chemicals used during the polishing process that you won't want on your skin. Finally, make sure your crystals don't have any sharp edges and won't go down the drain.

TRANQUILITEA TO BALANCE EMOTIONS & CALM NERVES

It may require a bit more effort to mix up a magickal brew than to use a store-bought tea bag, but there's just something about blending tea yourself that feels much more magickal. In this blend, lemon balm lends its stability, chamomile and lavender work in harmony to invoke relaxation, and passion-flower and rose offer loving vibrations. Let each ingredient infuse you with its energy while you sip and savor this ritual-made tea.

Materials

2 tablespoons dried chamomile

2 tablespoons dried lavender

2 tablespoons dried lemon balm
(or 2–3 fresh sprigs lemon balm)

2 tablespoons dried passionflower

2 tablespoons dried rose petals

Airtight container

Spoon or wand

Instructions

1. Add the chamomile, lavender, lemon balm, passionflower, and rose petals to the container.

2. Hold your hands over the container and charge it with your focused intention of balancing emotions and calming nerves.

3. Using a spoon or wand, stir the mixture clockwise seven times to invoke healing.

4. Place the spoon or wand in the center of the mixture and say:

   "So it is, tranquility is fulfilled,

   I've restored balance, for this is my will."

5. Store your tea blend in a cool, dark place.

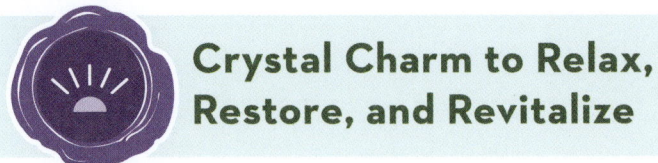

Crystal Charm to Relax, Restore, and Revitalize

After taking a shower or bath at night, sit comfortably in your bed. Take an amethyst in one hand, and a red jasper in the other. Visualize a warm light radiating from the minerals through your hands and filling your entire body. Feel calm, grounding energy filtering your thoughts and changing anything negative into useful, positive energy. Relax into this energy and, when you are ready, recite the following: "Radiant light, of divine glow, relax and restore above and below." Then place the crystals under your pillow. The next morning, run them under water to cleanse their energy. Repeat this charm as often as needed. It's a good idea to charge the crystals periodically under the full moon.

Charming a Worry Stone

Worry stones, also known as stress stones, are small, smooth stones that provide relief from stress and anxiety when you rub them. You can craft them from various materials; popular choices include amethyst, jasper, quartz, and other semi-precious gemstones. Some purchased worry stones feature a central indentation or groove for a better thumb fit, but any soothing stone that fits in your fingers will suffice.

Choose a stone that feels right to you, whether it is purchased or found, and then cleanse, bless, and dedicate it for this purpose. To do this, anoint the chosen stone with any anointing liquid in a clockwise spiral or other symbol that feels right to you. Bring your focused intention to communicate your desire to have the stone aid you. When using your worry stone, call upon the element of earth to ground and center your emotions around the worry. And remember to cleanse the stone weekly to release accumulated worries.

SERENITY BLOOM
POTION TO EASE ANGST

In this spell, centuries of serenity-packed wisdom come together in a single, spectacular combination. Whether you're seeking a moment of calm for yourself or looking to infuse your tools with an essence of serenity, this potion is your perfect partner to invoke peaceful moments. Use it as a body oil to bring about a peaceful night's sleep, rub it on your temples or between your brows in stressful moments, or use it to anoint magickal items in spells and rituals that call for calming energy.

Materials

Any combination of the following dried herbs (ideally the flower or leaves): calendula, chamomile, hops, jasmine, lavender, lemon balm, linden flower, passionflower, peony, rose, and valerian

Jar with lid

Grapeseed oil

Blue lace agate stone (optional)

⇛⇛ *Instructions* ⇚⇚

1. Take a few deep breaths and be sure that your energy is focused and grounded. If it helps, take a walk outside and let your bare feet touch the ground. You may even wish to play calming music while making this potion.

2. When you are ready, fill a mixing bowl with your desired dried herbs. You'll need enough to almost fill the jar.

3. With clean hands, combine the herbs in the bowl while visualizing yourself in a state of peace and calm. Continue moving the herbs, concentrating on the plant material cascading through your fingers as you pinch, sprinkle, and swirl it. Use your finger to draw a clockwise swirl to invoke tranquility and draw any other symbols or signs that feel calming to you. Keep your eyes open yet maintain a tranquil mind. This process should resemble a moving meditation, gradually leading you into a calm and relaxed trance-like state.

4. Once you feel that the mixture is completely infused with serenity, fill the jar, leaving some space free at the top.

5. Pour the grapeseed oil over the mixture, covering all plant material completely with oil.

6. Tightly secure the lid and label the jar, remembering to include the date.

7. Set the jar in a window, preferably north or south facing to avoid direct sunlight. To boost the calming energy, you can place a blue lace agate on top of the jar.

8. Shake the jar daily while thinking of calming and relaxing thoughts.

9. After 4 weeks, strain the mixture, discard the solids, and store the remaining oil in a cool, dark place. The potion can be used for up to one year, although it's a good idea to charge it regularly.

CALM WHISPER BAG TO REDUCE ANXIETY

You know those moments when excessive worrying, racing thoughts, and restless feelings just take over? Yeah, anxiety's got its grip on us. Trust me, I've felt it too, and I bet I'm not the only one. Now, let me introduce you to this spell bag—it's packed with some serious anti-anxiety energy. Self-cleansing selenite and amethyst bring the healing, with rose quartz playing emotional referee, clear quartz for centering, and black tourmaline for clearing tension.

Materials

Blue candle

Sewing pin or something sharp for etching

Serenity Bloom Potion (page 71) or lavender essential oil in a carrier oil

Dried chamomile, eucalyptus, lavender, and peppermint or spearmint

Coarse salt

Black tourmaline, clear quartz, amethyst, rose quartz, and selenite crystals

Blue, purple, or white cloth bag

⟶⟫⟩ *Instructions* ⟨⟨⟵

1. Dress the candle with the name of anything you wish to heal from in your life, such as stress, anxiety, tension, mood swings, doubt, or anger.

2. Anoint the candle with a few drops of Serenity Bloom Oil or lavender oil, moving from the base of the candle away from you and avoiding the wick.

3. Light the candle and place the herbs and crystals inside the bag while saying:

    "To gather and ease these emotions profound,

    grant me clarity where answers are found.

    Stress and tension, I bid you depart;

    replace with tranquility, a calm beating heart.

    I am free from restlessness, anxiety's chain;

    as I will, peace flows to me, without strain."

4. Let the candle burn all the way down, then keep the bag with you. When you are feeling added angst, squeeze the bag and inhale its calming aroma.

CELESTIAL EMBER FOR COURAGEOUS SELF-EMPOWERMENT

Whenever I'm craving that extra cosmic nudge and a shot of confidence, this spell is my go-to. It involves one of my all-time magickal favorites: dandelions. This little plant embodies the sun as it blooms, the moon as a puffball, and the stars in the form of countless seeds. But be prepared—the dandelion's name comes from the French *dent de lion*, which translates to "tooth of the lion." When you cast this spell, get ready to let the Universe hear you roar!

Materials

Orange candle

Tweezers or small tongs

Whole dried bay leaves

Permanent marker

Fireproof container

Dried dandelion seeds or flower

Cinnamon sticks

Fresh or dried ginger

Lemon or orange essential oil

Small decorative bowl

⇢⋙ Instructions ⋘⇠

1. Light the orange candle and focus your energy and intention on the warm flame as you feel a sense of power fill your body.

2. On the bay leaves, write down all that you want to embody. Use one bay leaf for each word or phrase to describe what you are seeking.

3. Use the tweezers or tongs to hold one of the bay leaves and, using the orange candle, carefully light it on fire. Continue to hold it while it burns, then place it in a fireproof container to turn into ash. Repeat with the remaining bay leaves.

4. Add the dandelion, cinnamon sticks, and ginger to the container with the ash. (You'll need enough of the herbs to fill the decorative bowl.)

5. Add a few drops of the essential oil and mix everything together.

6. Hold your hands over your heart and say:

    "I am loved, I am powerful, I am joy, I am enough."

7. Meditate on this energy for as long as you can while the candle burns.

8. Pour the mixture from the fireproof container into the decorative bowl and place it where you get ready in the morning to infuse you with its bold energy.

SPELL TO DISPEL SELF-DOUBT

Feeling like an imposter? You're in good company, my friend. I'm here to tell you that you're not alone. When that little voice inside your head won't stay quiet, turn to this spell to help overcome your self-doubt. A few strands of your hair serve as a personal-tie item to spiritually connect you to the magickal working. Raspberry leaf and cinquefoil come to your rescue with their notably protective aspects, while nettle, salt, and garlic dispel what does not serve you.

Materials

Pen and paper

Few strands of your hair

Dried cinquefoil, nettle, and raspberry leaf

Salt

Clove of garlic

Instructions

1. Write your name in the middle of a piece of paper.

2. Place your hair over your name and sprinkle the cinquefoil, nettle, raspberry leaf, and salt over it.

3. Place the clove of garlic over your hair, then repeatedly fold the paper away from you, turning it as necessary, so that it becomes a secured package.

4. Hold the package in your left hand and flick it three times with your right hand while saying:

   "To dispel self-doubt and set me free,

   my true-self I'll forever be."

5. Sleep with the pouch under your pillow until the next full moon, then bury it, or safely burn it and bury the ashes in your yard or in a potted plant.

Charm Bag to Banish Bad Habits

When the moon is waning, take a pouch or cloth and add to it angelica root, cinquefoil, horseradish root, and Solomon's seal, as well as black obsidian, labradorite, and selenite crystals. Write your name on a piece of paper and add it to the pouch with a strand of your hair. Carry this simple charm bag with you to help banish any bad habits for good. And remember to cleanse it regularly, as it will absorb energy and act as a mirror to your inner self.

Calming Essence Relaxation Incense Blend

Did you know you can create your own incense blends? This one is perfect for use in spells with calming intentions. With a mortar and pestle or in an electric coffee grinder, combine dried lavender, mallow, passionflower, and tulsi until you have a fragrance you like and approximately ½ cup of ground herbs. Then add 2½ tablespoons of makko powder and a few drops of water to create a workable paste. Shape this paste into cones or sticks. Allow them to dry completely before burning them as a soothing incense.

Incense through the Ages

The history of incense can be traced back to ancient civilizations like Egypt and Mesopotamia, where it played a central role in religious rituals. The Middle Ages saw it continue to flourish in Christian religious ceremonies, especially within enduring traditions associated with the gifts of frankincense and myrrh presented at the birth of Jesus. Burning incense has also long been a common practice within Chinese Taoism and Buddhism. India embraces incense as a vital component of Hindu rituals and Ayurvedic medicine, while Greece and Rome adopted it through trade with the East. Many indigenous tribes also have a tradition of using aromatic plants and resins in their ceremonies. With such a rich history, it is no wonder that incense became the symbol of purification and spirituality that we witches know today.

EMOTIONAL BALANCING SPELL TO DISSIPATE ANGER & ANGST

This spell can provide swift relief for someone experiencing inner turmoil—or for someone who simply has a hot temper. Anger and angst can be the result of imbalances in elemental energies within oneself. To restore balance, this spell uses the calm and cleansing influence of water to temper fire's intensity. And because fire's vitality can only be sustained with support from the element of air, you'll trap the flame inside the glass, causing the flame—and the negative emotions it represents—to extinguish itself. Salt serves as the stabilizing element, grounding the entire working to harmonize the energies.

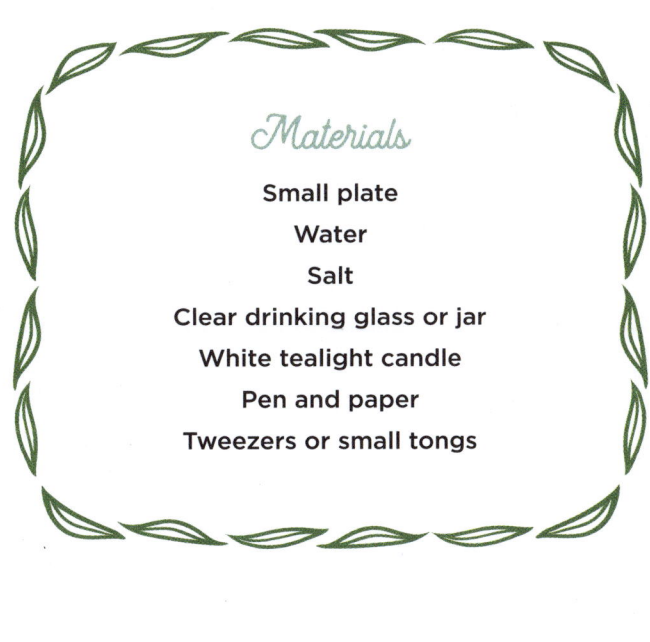

Materials

Small plate

Water

Salt

Clear drinking glass or jar

White tealight candle

Pen and paper

Tweezers or small tongs

⇢≫≫ Instructions ⟪⟪⟪⇠

1. Place the plate on your working surface and add enough water to cover the entire bottom of the plate. Then sprinkle the salt into the water.

2. Place the tealight in the center of the plate and light it. (Make sure the water isn't high enough to extinguish the flame.)

3. As the candle burns, use the paper and pen to write out what emotion you want to dissipate. Take some time to think about other feelings that might be behind the anger or angst that you are feeling.

4. Using the tweezers or tongs to hold the paper, carefully light it from the tealight's flame and let the ashes fall into the water on the plate. Allow the paper to burn completely.

5. While the tealight is still lit, say:

   "Earth, strong and grounded I will forever be;

   air, clear my mind, now my thoughts are free;

   water, wash away anger's fiery burn;

   with balance and harmony, tranquility returns."

6. Place the mouth of the drinking glass or jar over the tealight, watching as the flame, which represents anger and angst, is extinguished.

7. Discard the tealight and flush the water, ash, and salt mixture down the toilet.

SADNESS & MELANCHOLY BANISHING SPELL

The first time I realized that I could use magick to help me through sadness, I felt immediate relief. While I knew I couldn't solve all my problems with the wave of a wand, I also felt like I could do *something*, however small, to move forward. In that moment, I was reminded of the unending cycle where new life emerges from a single seed, growing from the ground up. In that spirit, this spell combines the healing power of rowan with the stability of earth energy to banish sadness and promote healing. If you can't find rowan, lavender will work. You'll also need to dig a hole in the dirt, but you can use a potted plant if you don't have access to a spot of land. This is a beautiful opportunity to transform your sadness by planting something new.

Materials

Nontoxic marker and paper

Small cup or bowl of water

Potted plant (optional)

Dried leaves or sticks of rowan

Clear quartz or smoky quartz stone

⇶ Instructions ⇷

1. Using the nontoxic marker, write down your feelings on a small piece of paper. Be honest and detailed about your emotions in your words.

2. Fold the paper away from you so that it is small enough to fit in the cup or bowl of water.

3. Place the paper into the water and watch as the water consumes it. Visualize your emotions being cleansed by the water while also knowing they will be used to benefit your future happiness.

4. Dig a hole in the ground or in the soil of a potted plant (without disturbing the plant, if it's already established).

5. Pull the paper out of the water and place it in the bottom of the hole while focusing on the energy of planting new seeds. Then add the dried rowan to the hole.

6. Cover the paper and rowan with soil, take a deep breath, exhale, and say:

   "By earth's stability and air's gentle breeze,

   with these soothing waters, my turmoil is at ease."

7. Pour the water over the soil as if you were watering seeds of happiness and growth.

RITUAL FOR RELEASING PAST TRAUMAS & GRIEF

The moon holds symbolic significance as a representation of emotional cleansing, which means that embracing moonlight's radiance can aid in your intentions for healing. This spell taps into the moon's transformative power through the color blue, which corresponds with water and its tides. Plant allies like wood betony and hyacinth provide spiritual resilience and support, paving the way for the nurturing guidance of lavender and gardenia. And a personal-tie item—such as, a few strands of hair, or even a shirt button—energetically links an individual (you or someone else) to the working. To amplify this spell's effectiveness, perform it during a full moon.

Materials

Blue candle

Sewing pin or something sharp for etching

5 x 5-inch black or blue cloth square

Permanent marker

Dried cypress, gardenia, hyacinth, lavender, rose petals, and wood betony

Personal-tie item

String or cord

⤜⤜⤜ Instructions ⤛⤛⤛

1. Dress the blue candle by etching into it words that describe what you want to release and heal from. Then light it and set it to the side.

2. Place the cloth on your working surface and, in the center, draw a symbol that represents transformation, such as the moon, a flower, or a butterfly.

3. Add the cypress, gardenia, hyacinth, lavender, rose petals, and wood betony to the center of the cloth over your drawing.

4. On top of the herbs, place your personal-tie item.

5. Hold your hands over the working and pour all of your grief, emotions, and feelings into it. If tears fall, allow them to.

6. Once you feel ready, drip the melted wax of the blue candle over the working. Visualize the blue wax as water, washing away all of your sorrow and heartache.

7. When the wax has cooled, gather the corners of the cloth to create a bundle, and use the string or cord to tie it together.

8. Allow the candle to burn out and the healing bundle to charge under the full moon, if you can.

9. Carry the healing bundle with you. If ever you need a little extra support, give it a gentle squeeze.

ALCHEMICAL LUNAR RITUAL FOR SHADOW WORK

This three-part ritual is designed to guide you in harnessing the lunar phases' power to transmute your shadows (the dark, unexplored parts of yourself) into positive actions. You'll begin a day or two before the new moon, during the last moments of the waning-crescent moon—a phase sometimes called the "dark moon." During this time, you will journal for self-reflection. On the new moon, you will set intentions and leverage the grounding energy of the earth for long-term benefits. As the full moon approaches, you will use candle magick to harness the full moon's energy and illuminate your shadows. If there is anything holding you back, you will use the power of fire to burn it away, casting it to the wind and the element of air. Finally, you will tap into the transformative energy of water to integrate these aspects of yourself into a healthy and balanced whole.

Materials

Journal

Pen or pencil

Paper

White or blue candle

Tweezers or small tongs

Fireproof vessel

Jar of drinking water with lid

Black obsidian, labradorite, and malachite stones

⇥ *Instructions: Part 1* ⇤

1. Begin with self-reflection during the dark moon. Think about what areas of your life feel the most challenging right now, and what recurring patterns, behaviors, or reactions you want to change. In your journal, answer these questions:

   "What are my triggers?" (These represent your strong, intense, emotional reactions and responses.)

   "What beliefs or patterns have been holding me back?" (These represent your unhealthy routines, pessimistic thoughts, or undesirable patterns.)

   "How do I project this onto the world?" (This represents the facades you present and the ways you interact with others that serve as veils to conceal your true self.)

2. Tune into your emotions and the issues that bring up strong reactions. This will help you determine where to set your focused intention. Allow any emotions that come up during this process to flow.

⇥ *Part 2* ⇤

1. On the night of the new moon, set clear intentions for your work moving forward. In your journal, define in detail what you hope to achieve and the changes you want to make in your life.

2. Write down your intentions on a separate piece of paper and bury it in the ground or in a potted plant. As you do this, imagine you are planting a seed of intention.

⇥ *Part 3* ⇤

1. On the night of the full moon, light the candle and reflect on your journaling from the dark moon. Visualize the candle illuminating your inner shadows while taking a moment to focus on the flame and the intentions you've set. Think about how you can accept and integrate shadow aspects of yourself in a healthy and balanced way. Add these thoughts to your journal.

2. On a separate piece of paper, write down your fears, negative beliefs, unhealthy patterns, and any other shadows that are holding you back. Then, using the tweezers or tongs to hold the paper, light it from the candle's flame and let it burn into the fireproof vessel.

3. Scatter the ashes to the wind to release the shadows while saying:

> "I release you.
>
> I appreciate the lessons you've taught,
>
> but you no longer have power here."

4. Remove the lid from the jar of water, hold the jar with both hands, and bring it to your heart.

5. Whisper into the water how you intend to accept and integrate your shadows in a healthy and balanced way. Replace the lid and set it out under moonlight to charge alongside the black obsidian, labradorite, and malachite.

6. Allow the candle to burn out. In the morning, drink the water and place the stones on your journal to seal your intentions.

What Is Shadow Work?

Shadow work is a concept developed by psychiatrist Carl Jung. It involves the exploration, acknowledgment, and integration of your unconscious psyche, which comprises hidden, repressed, or denied aspects of yourself. The concealed elements are often called "shadows," and they include thoughts, emotions, beliefs, and behaviors that you may not even be aware of or that you are not comfortable acknowledging.

Chapter 5

Health
&
Healing

My family was always rich in country remedies, superstitions, old wives' tales, and folk practices. Later in life, while learning about traditional medicine and herbalism, magick clicked for me. Green witches, like other folk practitioners, use common, easy-to-find ingredients, often tied to the region. In natural magick, you can enhance healing by weaving remedies with spells and rituals. But keep in mind that the healing spells, charms, and rituals in this section are crafted for magickal purposes, not medical ones. They are intended to assist the healing energy around you and may spiritually complement physical and mental healthcare. Please seek professional medical care when necessary.

ACCESSORY CHARGING STATION FOR GENERAL WELL-BEING

You have a charging station for your phone and electronic accessories. Now let's create a charging station for your magick. This little gem of a spell will not only cleanse but also recharge your magickal items, like bracelets and necklaces, as you snooze peacefully. The key is a custom sigil or symbol that corresponds with balance and well-being in all aspects of life. Crystals with energies that align with your intentions and desires boost the whole working. Choose the crystals for your charging station based on the energy with which you want to infuse your spell. (See page 214 for a wide variety of options.) Just swap them out as your energy ebbs and flows. And for an extra touch of magick, you can use the Botanical Shielding Oil (page 57), Abundance & Blessings Oil (page 114), or Multipurpose Moonlight Cleansing & Blessing Essence (page 36) as your anointing oil.

Materials

Pen and paper

Decorative plate

Anointing liquid

Any combination of amethyst, black tourmaline, bloodstone, carnelian, clear quartz, garnet, hematite, red jasper, rose quartz, selenite, smokey quartz, and tiger's eye stones

1. Create a sigil or symbol that corresponds with your intentions. (You can create more than one.) Using the pen, draw your sigil(s) or symbol(s) on the paper.

2. Anoint the four corners of the paper and place it where you intend to put your charging station.

3. Place the plate on top of the paper and use the anointing liquid and your finger to draw the same sigil on the plate.

4. Anoint the perimeter of the plate clockwise three times. Then use your hands to energetically push your intention into the plate.

5. Place each crystal you've chosen on the plate, one at a time, while verbally stating its intended purpose. (For example, you could say, "Hematite for concentration and focus.")

6. After you've assembled the working, place the magickal objects you wish to charge on the plate. Holding your hands over them, seal your energy and intention by saying:

    "As the day and night in rhythm flow,

    my life's energies align, balance, and grow."

7. Leave the objects to charge overnight, or perform a quick refresher by allowing your items to charge for a few minutes at any time throughout the day.

EMBER ELIXIR TO INCREASE WELLNESS

This elixir is jam-packed with fiery energy. You can use it for anointing during healing rituals when you want to expedite healing or invoke the essence of fire. However, it is most helpful as a wellness drink. You can take a quick shot of it from a tiny glass daily to keep your fire burning. But, personally, I prefer to mix it into a salad dressing. The ingredients need to ferment, though, so make sure you whip this elixir up a few weeks before you need it.

Materials

1 horseradish root, chopped

1 ginger root, chopped

3 turmeric roots, chopped

1 onion, peeled and roughly chopped

1 unpeeled orange, sliced

1 unpeeled lemon, sliced

16 garlic cloves, peeled

2–4 jalapeño peppers, sliced

Handful of fresh rosemary, sage, and thyme

Large jar with noncorrosive lid

Raw honey

Raw apple cider vinegar

Airtight container (optional)

1. Add the horseradish, ginger, turmeric, onion, orange, lemon, garlic, jalapeños, rosemary, sage, and thyme to the jar. As you do this, focus on the smell and heat of each ingredient. Envision that you are packing the jar full of fiery embers that will burn away unwellness.

2. Pour ⅛ to ¼ cup of the honey into the jar while thinking of its soothing and healing properties. Visualize it cleansing away unwanted energy and bringing sweetness to your health.

3. Pour the apple cider vinegar over the mixture, focusing on the vinegar's purifying properties, until all solids are covered.

4. Secure the lid and then shake the jar while holding your intention to seal the spell.

5. Store your brew in a cool, dark place, such as a cupboard, and shake your intention into it daily for 4 weeks.

6. After 4 weeks, strain the mixture to create your elixir and discard the solids. Store the elixir in an airtight container (or the same jar) for up to one year.

Sage Honey to Ward Against Illness

Sage honey is an age-old remedy that works for any number of ills. Honey boasts a rich history of healing that spans millennia and cultures. This natural sweetener is cherished not only for its taste but also for its remarkable medicinal properties. It can be used to soothe a sore throat, ward off infection, or treat a burn. Sage, with its anti-inflammatory and antioxidant benefits, has also been venerated in both magickal and medicinal practices. It's known for its ability to ease a cough, improve memory, and put a stop to excessive sweating.

To create your sage honey, add enough chopped fresh sage to a lidded jar to fill it one-quarter of the way. Next, cover the sage completely with honey, filling the jar to the brim while concentrating on your intention of warding off illness. Allow the mixture to rest in a cool, dark place for 2 to 4 weeks. You can incorporate the finished product into your tea, use it in your cooking, or add it to a healing spell.

Trinity Charm for General Healing

You truly can't surpass the effectiveness of the classic healing combination of amethyst, bloodstone, and clear quartz crystals. According to legend, amethyst is the ultimate stone for relieving physical, emotional, and psychological distress. Bloodstone, believed to enhance immunity and strength, has been revered for its healing properties since ancient times and is often used in amulets. Clear quartz offers amplification and balance. Create a simple charm using this powerful trio by placing them in a drawstring pouch, holding it, and envisioning yourself bathed in healing light. Then gently pass the bag over any area of illness and sleep with it beneath your pillow. In the morning, cleanse the stones. You can repeat this as often as you like and even perform this healing charm for a friend or loved one.

Nocturnal Nectar for a Healing Slumber

Whether I am having trouble falling asleep, feeling restless in the night, or even seeking deeper sleep for dream work, this brew never lets me down. To make it, add ½ teaspoon of each of the following herbs to a tea bag or food-safe pouch and steep it in boiling water for 5 minutes: chamomile, catnip, mugwort, oatstraw, rose petals, rosemary, skullcap, and yarrow. Each herb used in this blend possesses distinct magickal properties linked to love, joy, relaxation, protection, prosperity, divination, and dream work. After steeping, strain the mixture, then drink it as a tea or add it to your bath. You can also make this into a pillow spray by adding a few drops of a favorite essential oil. Combine it with the Witch's Prophesy Pillow (page 192) for extra-potent intuitive insights.

SAPPHIRE WATER FOR HEALING & PROTECTION

From the depths of the ocean to the endless expanse of the sky, blue is the color of boundless peace and healing. This spell taps into its therapeutic power to create a multitasking elixir. Often crafted from locally sourced ingredients, fragrance waters like this one have been integral to magickal practices across generations. The essential oils used in this recipe don't just impart a vibrant and earthy aroma with a subtle hint of spice, they also carry energetic qualities that amplify the intentions of healing and protection. Use this healing water in baths and hair rinses, to soak your feet or wash ailing areas, as a soothing spray, or in a compress.

Materials

Quart jar with lid

3½ cups water

2 tablespoons dried blue butterfly pea flower or 5 drops blue food coloring

Glycerin

Any combination of the following essential oils: bergamot, cinnamon, clove, lavender, lemon, orange

Instructions

1. Boil the water, then remove it from the heat and let the blue butterfly pea flower steep for 5 minutes. Then strain the liquid into the jar. (If using food coloring instead, simply add it to distilled water—no need to boil or strain.)

2. Add a few drops of glycerin to the mixture, followed by 2 to 5 drops of each essential oil.

3. Close the jar and shake in your focused intention for healing and protection.

4. Use this healing water immediately or place it under the full moon (for healing and protection) or waning moon (for repelling unwanted things) to charge it with the moon's energy. It will keep for up to 3 months at room temperature or up to 6 months when refrigerated.

COOLING BRAIN BALM TO BOOST MEMORY & RELIEVE HEADACHES

When I was little, my mom was known for being able to "pull out" a headache. She never fully explained how she did it, only saying that it was something she learned from her grandmother. I remember her moving her hands over my head slowly as if gathering my hair. The next thing I knew, the headache was gone.

While I never quite figured out her technique, I have come to learn that there are many ways to move the energy of an ache. One of my favorite ways is with this cooling balm, which can help boost your memory and melt away migraines. You'll be using an incredible combination of herbs that help soothe and calm the mind while also stimulating healing and memory. To make this balm, you'll need to create a double boiler to heat the ingredients slowly. You can make one by filling a large pot with 1 to 2 inches of water and placing a smaller pot or heatproof bowl inside. Add your ingredients to the smaller pot while the water outside of it, in the larger pot, slowly heats and melts them.

Materials

Quart jar with lid

2½ tablespoons dried blessed thistle

2½ tablespoons dried comfrey

2½ tablespoons dried lavender

2½ tablespoons dried rosemary

2½ tablespoons dried spearmint

1½ cups olive oil or grapeseed oil

1 cup coconut oil

5 tablespoons beeswax or calendula pellets

1 (16-ounce) jar with lid or 2 (8-ounce) jars

Lavender, rosemary, and spearmint
essential oils (optional)

➳ Instructions ⤳

1. Make the oil infusion by adding the blessed thistle, comfrey, lavender, rosemary, and spearmint to the quart jar. Don't forget to communicate your focused intention to your ingredients.

2. Pour the olive or grapeseed oil over the herbs until they are completely covered.

3. Put the lid on the jar and store it in a cool, dark place for 2 weeks. Check on it and shake your intention into it daily.

4. After 2 weeks, strain the solids from the oil and discard them.

5. To a double boiler set to low heat, add the coconut oil, beeswax pellets, and 1 cup of your strained oil infusion.

6. Let the mixture melt and blend as you hold your hands over it and say:

   "A memory sharp and a peaceful mind."

7. After the mixture has melted completely, remove it from the heat and add 1 drop each of lavender essential oil, rosemary essential oil, and spearmint essential oil, if desired. Stir the mixture before pouring it into the storage jars.

8. Dab some of this balm on your temples or rub it into a sore neck as needed.

When I feel the early signs of a cold or a minor illness, and I want to nip it in the bud before it gets worse, I always turn to onions. The practice of placing raw, cut-up onions around your home as a healing remedy may date back to the 1500s. In addition, recent studies suggest that onions are high in vitamins and compounds thought to boost immunity and aid in overall health. This is a beautiful example of sympathetic magick and how a magickal ingredient's energetic properties mirror its physical healing properties. This spell boosts that magick with herbs and elements that bring harmony to your healing.

Materials

1 onion

Salt

Ground ginger

Dried chamomile

Caraway seeds

5 small plates

Instructions

1. Before going to sleep at night, cut an onion into five rounds. Put each round on a plate and sprinkle with salt, ginger, chamomile, and caraway.

2. Place one round (on a plate) in each of the four corners of your bedroom and one under your bed. (But if you have pets, make sure your onions are inaccessible or skip this spell.)

3. Lay down and, just before you go to sleep, say:

   "By earth, by air, by fire, by sea,

   let healing energy flow through me."

4. Visualize the onion slices being connected by a blue light that forms a pentacle (or other symbol that feels protective to you) around your body.

5. Sleep in this healing, protective light. When you awaken in the morning, throw the onions away.

Chapter 6

Career
&
Productivity

When I say this chapter is about maximizing efficiency and growth and improving work-life balance, I mean it! Everyone is looking to enhance their career in some way. It doesn't matter if you are seeking recognition, a more positive environment, or to develop your skills, each spell here has been carefully crafted to empower you to get the most fulfillment from your professional journey.

SPELL FOR WORK-LIFE BALANCE

Whether you love your job or have been feeling burnt out for too long, everyone can benefit from better work-life balance. This spell promotes harmony during chaotic times and can be performed whenever you need it most, but it's even more powerful during a full moon. Using sage offers purification and balances energies, while chamomile brings luck and love. Earthy patchouli oil keeps you rooted, and obsidian helps dispel negativity.

Materials

Dried sage and chamomile

Plate

Small dropper bottle

Olive oil

Patchouli essential oil

2 polished obsidian stones

➤➤ Instructions ◄◄

1. Sprinkle the dried sage and chamomile onto your plate. Move your hands over the herbs three times in a counterclockwise motion while saying:

   "From chaos and discord,

   I now break free,

   In perfect balance,

   I shall be."

2. Move your hands three times in a clockwise motion while saying:

   "With sage and chamomile,

   I restore the balance forevermore."

3. Fill the small bottle with olive oil, add 5 drops of patchouli essential oil, and shake it up.

4. Use the oil to anoint both obsidians, swirling it evenly.

5. Hold one stone in each hand and focus on how you will feel once your work and life are balanced. Then place the obsidians in the middle of the dried herbs.

6. Use the oil to anoint yourself by drawing three clockwise circles over the center of your forehead and three clockwise circles over the center of your chest. Then say:

   "With focused mind and spirit aligned,

   emotional balance I now find."

7. Leave the working to sit overnight. In the morning, gather the herbs and sprinkle them over your walkway, sidewalk, or driveway. Place one obsidian where you work, and the other in a safe place at home. Use the oil to anoint yourself anytime you need a little extra help with work-life balance.

SPELL TO STOP SELF-SABOTAGE & INCREASE POTENTIAL

Acorns symbolize incredible potential. Although they are small in size, they contain the ability to grow into mighty oak trees, which are often associated with strength, endurance, and resilience. Therefore, acorns can represent the idea that even small and humble beginnings can develop into something powerful and substantial. These symbols of growth, patience, and the inner strength needed to persevere through challenges can help you achieve great things when combined with a bit of candle magick, the power of the elements, and a carnelian stone for motivation and creativity.

Materials

Orange or gold candle

Several acorns

Small bowl of soil or salt

Small bowl of water

Carnelian stone

Decorative cup or bowl

Instructions

1. Light the candle and focus on the flame. Visualize that it is your inner strength burning bright within you.

2. Take the acorns in your hands and blow gently on them to bless them with the element of air.

3. Roll the acorns over the soil or salt to bless them with the element of earth.

4. Hold the acorns in your hands over the candle flame so that you can feel the heat (being careful not to burn yourself) to bless them with the element of fire.

5. Sprinkle a few drops of water over the acorns to bless them with the element of water.

6. Add the acorns and carnelian to the cup or bowl and place it where you find yourself often. From time to time, stir the contents of the cup clockwise while holding your intentions to bring more energy into them.

EYES ON THE PRIZE TEA
FOR MEETING A DEADLINE

In need of a little bit of stamina for the final stretch? Whether you are studying for school or you've got a deadline for work, sipping this magickal brew can help you cross the finish line. The peppery-sweet flavor of tulsi keeps you rooted in your spiritual connection, while rosemary stimulates the senses. Adding galangal will light a fire under you; if you don't have any, ginger is a fine substitute.

Materials

3 teaspoons dried tulsi

3 teaspoons dried rosemary

1 teaspoon dried or 2 teaspoons fresh galangal

1 teaspoon cinnamon bark or
1 cinnamon stick broken into small pieces

1 teaspoon black peppercorns

5 cardamom pods, lightly crushed

Carnelian stone

Airtight container

Instructions

1. Place all ingredients, including the carnelian, in the airtight container.

2. Hold your hands over the mixture to charge it with your focused intention before saying:

    "With roots and leaves, a cup full of brilliance,

    I call to thee, to invigorate resilience.

    Provide me with stamina and grace

    as I cross the finish line and win this race."

3. When you need that energetic boost, add 1 teaspoon of the tea blend to 8 ounces of hot water. Let it steep for 5 to 7 minutes while holding the carnelian and again, bringing your focused intention to increase your resilience and stamina.

HARMONY IN THE WORKPLACE

When I need to balance the energy of a room, I call to the elements by using plants that correspond to each individual energy—oats for earth, sage for air, allspice for fire, and burdock root for water. These herbs can be fresh or dried. I've found that placing them in scallop shells works best for healing vibrations, but you could use little bowls instead.

Materials

4 scallop shells or small bowls

Salt

Pinch each of fresh or dried oats, sage, allspice, and burdock root

Instructions

1. Add a few pinches of salt to each scallop shell or bowl.

2. Add the oats to one shell, the sage to another, the allspice to another, and the burdock root to the last.

3. Place each shell in a corner of the building or office, ideally close to their corresponding directions (oats to the north, sage to the east, allspice to the south, and burdock root to the west), until you feel they have done their job.

GAIN RESPECT FOR EXPERTISE & INSIGHTS

There's nothing wrong with wanting to be recognized for your hard work and talents. If you're feeling a little overlooked, this spell will help others appreciate what you bring to the table. The book represents your knowledge, while rose and thyme help highlight your value. If you don't have a Tarot deck, you can use a photo of The Emperor card or a throne to symbolize authority. Using a tray to set up the spell makes for an easy transition.

Materials

Emperor Tarot card

Book

Tray

Fresh or dried rose petals and thyme

Pen and paper

Instructions

1. Before you go to bed at night, place the Tarot card inside the book in a random spot.

2. Set the book on the tray and spread the rose petals and thyme around the book while holding your intention.

3. Place the tray under your bed, then go to sleep.

4. When you awake the next morning, open the book to the page the Tarot card has marked and read whichever line first comes to your attention.

5. Write down that line on a piece of paper and carry it with you.

Writer's Flow Enchantment to Break Writer's Block

Writer's block affects writers of all experience levels and genres. Whether you're facing a blank page while writing a novel or anxious about choosing your words in an email, this little charm can help. I've made a habit of performing it every time I sit down to write. All you need is a sharpened and cleansed pencil. Hold it between your hands, focusing all your energy on it, and say:

> "Muse of words,
> I call to thee.
> Unblock my mind,
> set my thoughts free."

Use the charmed pencil to hold up your hair (I usually secure my hair with pins and hair ties first), or tuck it behind your ear, and keep it there while you work. When you are done, take it out and keep it in a safe place. Reactivate it as often as necessary by simply repeating the charm.

Charm for Finding Career Fulfillment

On a Sunday, etch the number "1," followed by your name, into a yellow candle. Place The World Tarot card on your working surface, then place the candle on top of the card. Set a malachite stone on the card, then light the candle. Bring your focused intention to the candle's flame, feeling its warmth grow and fill you with radiant, glowing energy. Focus on attracting what it is that you need to feel fulfilled by your career. Allow the candle to burn all the way down and extinguish itself.

SACRED KEY RITUAL TO UNLOCK CAREER OPPORTUNITIES

In times when you seek to open paths to greater career opportunities, this ritual is for you. In magick, keys symbolize the unlocking of hidden knowledge, mysteries, and gateways. They hold sacred significance to the goddess Hecate, who is closely associated with witchcraft, witches, magick, and sorcery. Basil, chamomile, cinnamon, and mint are all associated with luck, money, and abundance, while citrine, clear quartz, green aventurine, and pyrite assist with success, achievement, and prosperity. Once you've enchanted your key, add it to your wallet, purse, or keychain. Place the pouch or bundle of powerful ingredients at your desk or in your car, or carry it with you when you're headed into an important meeting.

Materials

Key

Large gold, orange, or green candle

Pouch or cloth and piece of string

Dried basil, chamomile, and mint

Ground cinnamon

Citrine, clear quartz, green aventurine, and pyrite stones

Candle snuffer or shot glass

⇢⟫⟫⟩ *Instructions* ⟨⟨⟨⟵

1. Use the key to carve the words "career opportunities" into the candle, followed by your name (whichever name you feel most connected to).

2. Light the candle, then place it off to the side of your working surface.

3. Lay the pouch or cloth out before you. Visualize success and career opportunities coming your way as you hold each ingredient in your hand and then place it in the pouch or on the cloth. Tap into the feeling of what it means to you to have your desires and needs met.

4. Close the pouch or gather the string around the cloth and tie it into a secure bundle. Then kiss your hand and touch the pouch or bundle two times. Say:

   "As I stand before the flame's gentle glow,

   I call upon energies that ebb and flow.

   With basil, chamomile, cinnamon, and mint,

   I summon good luck and success to imprint."

5. Kiss your hand, touch the pouch two times more, and say:

   "From earth, these herbs, gifts of nature's grace,

   grant me prosperity and a swift career pace.

   Citrine's glow, green aventurine's gleam,

   pyrite's spark, and clear quartz's dream."

6. Kiss your hand again, touch the pouch two final times, and say:

   "With this [color] candle's flickering light,

   I draw opportunities both day and night.

   May my path be clear, my purpose steadfast,

   building opportunities that grow and last."

7. Carefully bring the candle back out in front of you, gazing into the flame and focusing on its warmth.

8. Snuff out the flame using the snuffer or shot glass, then pass the key through the smoke while saying:

   "Blessed be, this spell is spun,

   as I will, it is done."

9. Add the key to your wallet, purse, or keychain. Place the pouch or bundle at your desk or in your car, or carry it with you when you're headed into an important meeting.

ATTRACT YOUR DREAM JOB

Are you searching for a new job or ready to take the next step in your career? I love this simple spell that packs a punch. It uses cloves to attract riches, poppy seeds and minerals to bring luck and money, and sunny flowers for inviting brighter days ahead.

Materials

Open container

Cloves

Poppy seeds

Fresh or dried sunflower, dandelion, or chamomile

Citrine (or clear quartz) and green jasper stones

Instructions

1. Place all ingredients in a cleansed container.

2. Hold your hands over the container while visualizing yourself in a new role. Really home in on how it feels to be in that position daily, and say:

   "You're the job of my dreams,

   everything that I seek.

   When I close my eyes,

   it's you that I see.

   With this charm,

   I draw you to me."

3. Keep the container at your desk or by your side when you are working on your résumé, searching for jobs, or preparing for an interview. You can also pour the mixture into a pouch and carry it with you on interviews.

BLESSING RITUAL FOR STARTING A NEW JOB OR CAREER PATH

Designed to foster success, fulfillment, and harmony on your new path, this ritual will infuse positive energy into a new job or career. A white or gold candle symbolizes the light you're inviting as basil and salt water bestow blessings and abundance. You can use any incense in this ritual, but I suggest Pathway to Prosperity Incense (page 118).

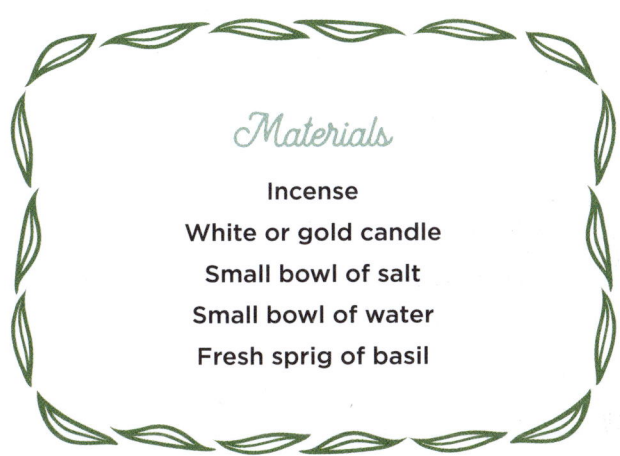

Materials

Incense

White or gold candle

Small bowl of salt

Small bowl of water

Fresh sprig of basil

⇢⟫ Instructions ⟪⇠

1. Light the incense and cleanse yourself by using your hands to direct the smoke over you. Visualize it as a waterfall, cleansing you of any career and money blocks.

2. Light the white or gold candle. Bring your focused intention to the light and the positive energy you're inviting.

3. Hold your hands safely over the candle's flame. As you feel its warmth, visualize success and fulfillment in this new journey.

4. Take a pinch of salt and add it to the bowl of water, stirring it clockwise three times.

5. Dip your fingers into the salt water and sprinkle a small amount around the candle. As you do this, say:

   "Blessed salt of the earth,

   fill my life with mirth.

   Concentrate this path before me,

   guide my steps and set me free."

6. Dip the sprig of basil into the salt water and sprinkle it gently over yourself. Holding the sprig between your hands, inhale its fragrance as you close your eyes and envision success and positive energy surrounding you.

   "With divine essence, I will find

   strength, perseverance, and peace of mind.

   With my power, I decree:

   Inspire this journey, blessed be!"

7. Let the candle burn down completely, or respectfully extinguish it and relight it consecutively with the same intention until it is finished. Discard the salt water but save the sprig of basil to keep at your desk or office.

Incantation for Inspiration

The Muses are nine goddesses in Greek mythology—the daughters of Zeus and Mnemosyne. They are often called upon to inspire artists, musicians, scholars, and poets. Each has a specific area of creativity or knowledge:

- Calliope: epic poetry

- Polyhymnia: sacred poetry

- Erato: romantic poetry

- Clio: historical inspiration

- Euterpe: music

- Terpsichore: dance

- Melpomene: poetic and theatrical tragedy

- Thalia: comedy

- Urania: astronomy

When you're in need of inspiration, you can call on any or all of them. Chant this incantation, then blow a kiss to the sky. You can also charm an object that you plan on wearing or keeping close to you while you work by reciting this incantation over it and blowing a kiss toward the object. Stack the odds in your favor by performing this on a Sunday, the day associated with the sun's fast-acting, fiery energy. Just say:

> "I call upon the essence of the Muse,
> I kiss my hand to you.
> Goddesses of Nine,
> keepers of the divine,
> daughters of Zeus,
> inspire my creation,
> infuse every vibration,
> ignite the synchronization
> of my imagination."

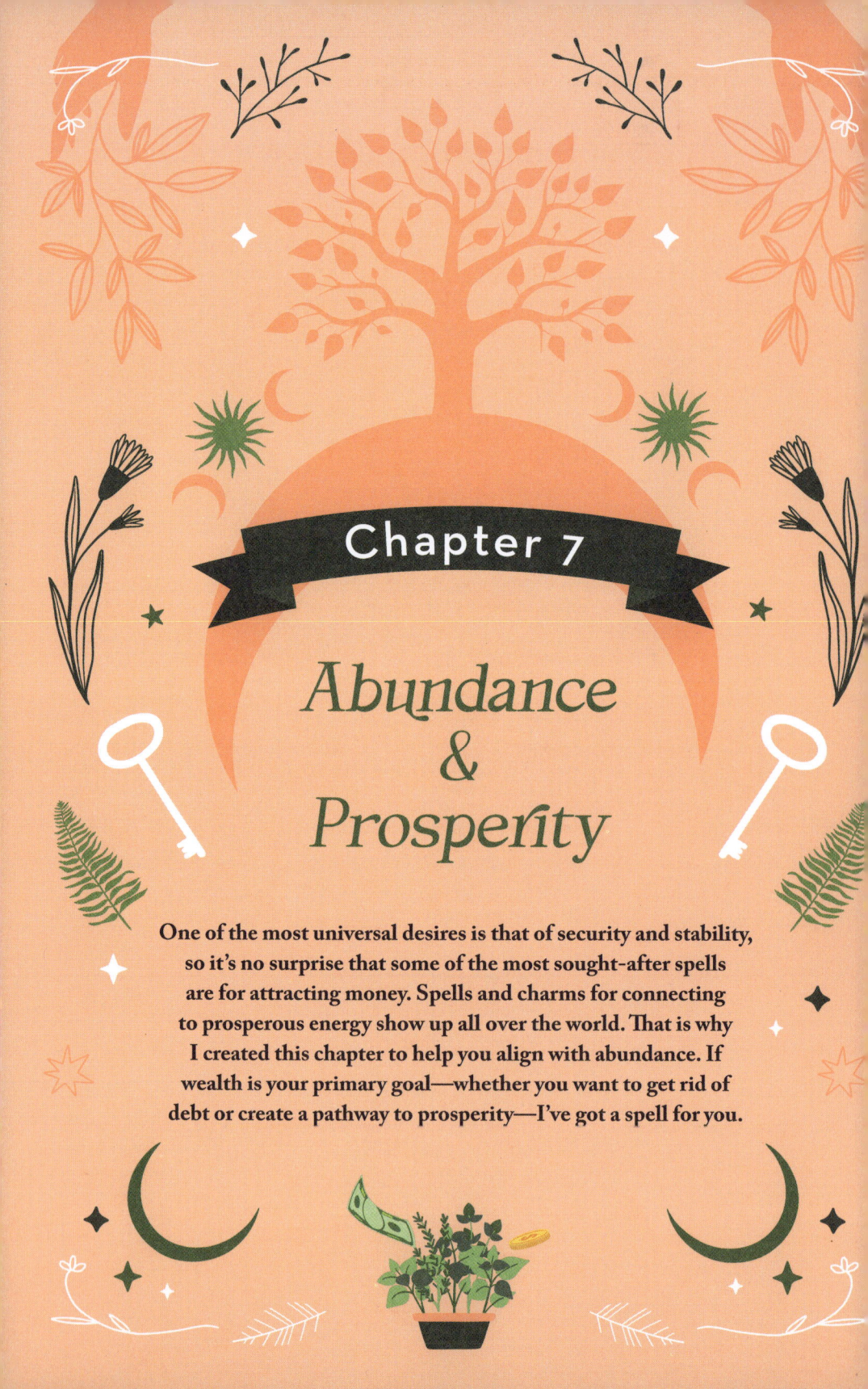

Chapter 7

Abundance & Prosperity

One of the most universal desires is that of security and stability, so it's no surprise that some of the most sought-after spells are for attracting money. Spells and charms for connecting to prosperous energy show up all over the world. That is why I created this chapter to help you align with abundance. If wealth is your primary goal—whether you want to get rid of debt or create a pathway to prosperity—I've got a spell for you.

SPELL TO CLEANSE YOURSELF OF BAD MONEY HABITS

Banish bad money management, careless spending habits, and overall unrewarding financial situations with this rejuvenating and purifying foot soak. You'll use salt to shield yourself from harmful influences, rosemary for clarity, sage to purify your ways, and mint to keep you alert.

Materials

Large bowl (to soak your feet)

Water to fill the bowl, heated to your preferred temperature

½ cup Epsom salt or sea salt

2 tablespoons dried rosemary

1 tablespoon dried sage

1 tablespoon dried mint

2 drops peppermint essential oil

Instructions

1. In the bowl, combine the salt with the herbs and mix the ingredients thoroughly.

2. Add the heated water to the mixture and stir.

3. Slip your feet into the mixture. As you soak, take deep breaths and allow the aromatic herbs to envelop you. Focus on an intention of relaxing, receiving clarity, and washing away the worldly behaviors that do not serve you.

4. Soak your feet for about 10 minutes. When you are finished, pour the water out of the bowl and down the drain to symbolize your bad habits being removed.

Abundance & Blessings Oil

To effortlessly draw money to you, fill a 2-ounce dropper bottle with almond oil, leaving a bit of space at the top. Then add the following essential oils: 5 drops of patchouli to attract wealth, 2 drops of cinnamon to increase success, 5 drops of bergamot for money, 5 drops of orange for joy, and 7 drops of chamomile for luck. Replace the top and shake in your focused intention. Use this oil to anoint yourself, candles, or other magickal tools.

Green Witch's Spell Paper to Attain Wealth

When performing rituals and spells, any kind of paper will do. But creating your own spell paper, infused with particular intentions, can give your workings some added oomph. This spell paper is perfect for anything involving abundance and manifestation. To make it, place pieces of paper in a single layer on a rimmed baking dish. Bring a pot of water to a boil, then turn off the heat and add the following: 3 tablespoons of green tea to energize your magick, a pinch of basil for money, a pinch of cinnamon to attract abundance, a pinch of spirulina for growth, and a pinch of chamomile for luck. Let this mixture steep for 15 minutes. Strain the solids from the mixture, then carefully pour the liquid over the baking sheet, covering the paper. Let the pieces of paper soak overnight, then carefully remove them from the water and lay them flat to dry for future use.

DEBT-BANISHING LUNAR ILLUMINATION

During the waning moon, when its energy decreases, is the perfect time for banishing things that do not serve you. In this spell, you'll banish debt by first placing a quarter tails up. Then, when the moon is waxing, you'll flip the quarter to invoke polarity and attract abundance. I suggest using Abundance & Blessings Oil (page 114) for this one, but olive oil will work, too.

Materials

Black candle

Sewing pin or something else sharp for etching

Quarter or other coin

Candle snuffer or shot glass

Gold candle

Anointing liquid

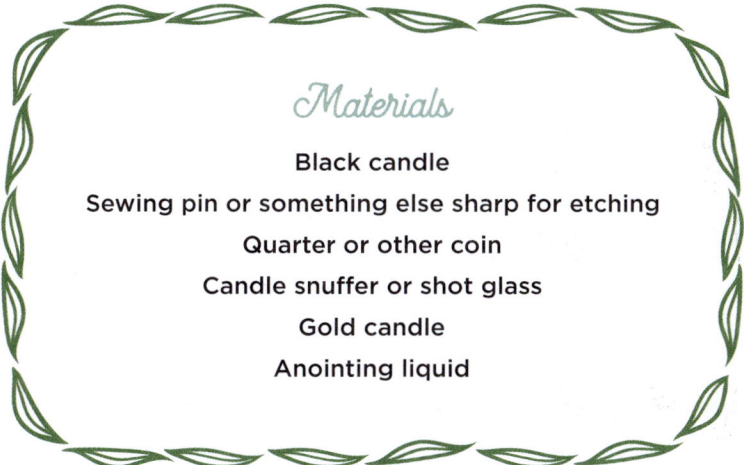

ᐳᐳᐳ Instructions ᐸᐸᐸ

1. During a waning moon, carve the amount of debt you want to banish into the black candle. (No need to anoint it.) You could also carve "bad spending habits" or "limiting beliefs."

2. Place the coin tails up, then set the black candle on top of it and light the candle.

3. While the candle burns, meditate on your debt melting away. Focus your intention on your spending habits and your fears and shadows surrounding money.

4. Let the candle burn for a few minutes, then extinguish it using a candle snuffer or shot glass.

5. Over the course of the waning moon, relight the black candle and meditate on your intention, ensuring that the candle burns all the way down before the new moon.

6. On the night of the new moon, anoint the gold candle, with the oil moving toward yourself, from the top to the bottom.

7. Flip the coin over to heads and place the gold candle on top of it.

8. Light the candle and focus your intention on abundance and blessings coming your way. After a few minutes, extinguish the candle.

9. Over the course of the new moon and waxing moon, relight the gold candle and meditate on your intention, ensuring that it burns all the way down before the full moon. Repeat this with the next moon cycle if you feel called to.

PROSPEROUS MONEY CRYSTAL MAGICK SCRUB

This mixture is loaded with spices and extracts aimed at repelling the bad and drawing in the good. I keep a jar of this hand scrub next to my kitchen sink and use it every time I wash my hands. Many spiritual beliefs associate the hands with receiving money, wealth, and abundance. By combining salt with sugar, you can purify and bless anything you touch—including money.

Materials

½ cup granulated sugar

¼ cup salt

1 teaspoon ground cinnamon

½ teaspoon ground ginger

½ teaspoon ground cardamom

¼ teaspoon ground cloves

¼ teaspoon ground nutmeg

¼ teaspoon vanilla extract

¼ cup almond oil

Airtight container

Instructions

1. In a large mixing bowl, combine the sugar, salt, cinnamon, ginger, cardamom, cloves, and nutmeg.

2. Mix them well, then use a finger to draw money signs in the mixture.

3. Pour the vanilla extract over the mixture, followed by the almond oil, then stir everything together until well combined. As you do this, bring your focused attention to attracting prosperity.

4. Pour the mixture into an airtight container and set it by your sink.

5. After washing your hands, scrub them with a quarter-sized amount of the mixture while saying:

   "Scrub away impurity, and bring to me prosperity."

Simple Money Charms

Money is the physical representation of abundant energy. To easily align with this energy, you can do a number of simple things:

- Arrange fresh basil, rosemary, mint, and/or chamomile in a vase and place it near your primary entrance.

- Carry the Ace of Pentacles, a piece of paper with the rune Fehu (ᚠ), a bay leaf with dollar signs drawn on it, or a citrine stone in your purse or wallet.

- Rub a bit of Abundance & Blessings Oil (page 114) between your palms before shaking hands in financial meetings. (Let it absorb first, though.)

- Chew on a whole clove before asking for a raise or meeting with a potential client.

- Draw a money sigil on a cinnamon stick and burn it to attract money fast. Toss sigil-inscribed cinnamon sticks into water to clear the emotions surrounding money or use them in an incense blend to earn money from your creative endeavors. Or, if you want long-term results, bury them.

Pathway to Prosperity Incense for Removing Money Blocks

Cleansing yourself and your workspace with this DIY incense regularly can help you remove money blocks. To an electric coffee grinder or mortar and pestle, add allspice, cinnamon bark, cloves, dried ginger, powdered pine gum, and vetiver root until you have a fragrance you like. Grind them into a fine powder until you have about ½ cup of the mixture. To that, add 2½ tablespoons of makko powder, a drizzle of honey, 7 drops of cedar essential oil, and a few drops of water until you have a workable paste. Shape this into cones or sticks and let them dry completely before burning.

FUNDAMENTAL MONEY MAGICK FOR WEALTH

This simple money spell uses one of my favorite magickal ingredients: sidewalk chalk. With it, you'll combine the alchemical symbol for the element of earth, which symbolizes stability and abundance, with the rune Fehu (ᚠ), which represents wealth. You'll also use an herb to help attract money. Chamomile is my favorite, but feel free to use yours. Some other possibilities include alfalfa, allspice, basil, bay leaves, bayberry, cinnamon, clove, dill, juniper, mint, nutmeg, patchouli, rosemary, and thyme.

Materials

Sidewalk chalk in white or green

Fresh or dried chamomile (or herb of your choice)

Instructions

1. Using the chalk on a paved surface, draw a circle large enough for you to stand inside of it.

2. Within that circle, draw the elemental symbol for earth: an inverted triangle with a horizontal line through it.

3. Within the symbol for earth, draw the rune Fehu (ᚠ).

4. Stand inside the circle and sprinkle the chamomile in a clockwise circle around yourself.

5. With your hands raised to the sky, chant three times:

   "From earth to sky,

   through land and sea,

   I attract abundance and prosperity."

SIMPLE CINNAMON SPELL FOR ABUNDANCE

Both the new moon and the first day of the month offer excellent opportunities for honoring the beginning of a cycle. It doesn't matter whether you align with the lunar cycle or your billing cycle; what truly matters is sustaining the energy. Cinnamon is believed to attract money directly into your home, so you should always keep a bit of this spice near your front door. While any pen or ink will get the job done in this spell, using Money Magnet Ink (opposite) can enhance your chances of success.

Materials

Pen or money ink

Small piece of paper

Cinnamon stick

Anointing liquid

String

Instructions

1. Using the pen or money ink, write on the paper: "Drawing and attracting, I magnetize abundance appearing before my eyes."

2. Anoint the paper by drawing three clockwise circles with the anointing liquid, then wrap the paper around the cinnamon stick, folding it toward you if necessary. Secure it by using the string to tie a bow.

3. Place the cinnamon stick above your primary entrance until the next new moon or the first day of the month. Then untie and unroll the paper, anoint it, wrap and tie it around the cinnamon stick again, and place it back above your door.

4. Repeat this ritual monthly until the cinnamon stick and paper are worse for wear. Then burn the bundle and start a fresh one, sprinkling some of the ashes of the old one into the new paper with the cinnamon.

MONEY MAGNET INK

Magickal inks amplify your intentions when writing on spell papers. Use this one, made with green spirulina, to nourish and attune your personal energy, transforming you into a money magnet. A touch of honey keeps it vibrant and sweet.

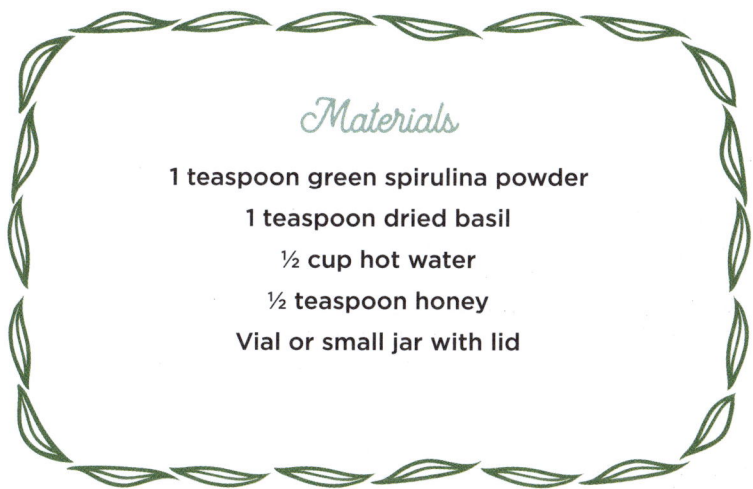

Materials

1 teaspoon green spirulina powder

1 teaspoon dried basil

½ cup hot water

½ teaspoon honey

Vial or small jar with lid

Instructions

1. Steep the basil in hot water for 5 minutes, then mix in the rest of the ingredients until well combined.

2. Transfer to a vial or jar and store, covered, in the fridge for up to 3 months.

3. To use this ink, dip the tip of a feather, quill, twig, paintbrush, or pen in it and inscribe your incantations on the desired paper.

GREEN GRAINS OF PLENTY FOR ABUNDANCE

This mixture may be simple, but it's full of powerful ingredients. Rice, long regarded as a symbol of a bountiful harvest, carries prosperous energy. When bergamot touches money, it ensures its return. And cedar attracts money when placed in your purse or wallet. All of these combine in this magickal blend that gets its signature color from spirulina, bringing strength and vitality to the mix. (In a pinch, a few drops of green food coloring can work instead.) You can use this mixture in any spell for wealth or abundance, but see "Simple Charms for Green Grains of Plenty" (opposite) for a few ideas.

Materials

1 cup white rice

1 teaspoon green spirulina powder

½ teaspoon water

7 drops bergamot essential oil

4 drops cedar essential oil

Plastic zip-top bag

Parchment-lined baking sheet

Jar with lid

Instructions

1. Add the rice, spirulina powder, water, and essential oils to the plastic bag.

2. Seal the bag tightly and shake it to combine the mixture.

3. Once all ingredients are well incorporated, spread the mixture on the parchment-lined baking sheet.

4. Set the baking sheet out in the sun to charge the mixture with fire energy until it is completely dry. Store it in a lidded jar until needed.

Simple Charms for Green Grains of Plenty

The possibilities for using the Green Grains of Plenty blend are truly endless, so don't hesitate to let your imagination run wild. Here are a few creative ways that I personally favor when it comes to harnessing this blend's potential:

- Add a layer of Green Grains to a plate and set your wallet or money on top to charge it with abundant energy.

- Fill a pouch or sachet with the grains and carry it with you throughout the day.

- Fill a small bottle with the grains and keep it on your desk, giving it a gentle shake whenever you need to reestablish your connection with abundance.

Pouch of Plenty for Prosperity and Abundance

When I want to ensure a prosperous flow of energy, I create this potent little charm. Gather a pouch or sachet (or a small piece of cloth and a cord) and place chamomile, mint, citrine, and pyrite inside. Next, draw a sigil on a piece of paper, personalizing it to your intentions, and add it to the pouch. For an extra boost, consider anointing the sigil with Abundance & Blessings Oil (page 114) and using Money Magnet Ink (page 121) to draw the sigil. You can also amplify the charm's effectiveness by incorporating money rice, such as Green Grains of Plenty (opposite). (Common grains such as corn or oatmeal will also work.) Carry this pouch with you, especially when you are dealing with financial matters or while you're at work, to serve as a talisman to attract prosperity and positive energy into your life.

SPICE DIVINATION TO AID IN FINANCIAL DECISIONS

I know I'm not the only one—few things make people more anxious than anticipating financial decisions. When you've got a hard choice to make in the realm of money matters, use this spicy divination trick. Cinnamon vibrates with abundance and prosperity.

Materials

3 cinnamon sticks

Permanent marker

Cup

Cloth napkin, altar cloth, or scarf

→)))→ Instructions ←(((←

1. Cleanse all of your materials with incense, then lay the cloth out on your surface.

2. Using a permanent marker, draw a check mark to represent a positive outcome on one of the cinnamon sticks and an "X" on another to represent a negative outcome. Leave the third cinnamon stick blank.

3. Add the cinnamon sticks to the cup, place your hand over it, and shake the contents while focusing on your question.

4. When you feel ready, turn the cup and spices out onto the cloth.

5. Interpret the cinnamon sticks by seeing which one is closest to you. If the cinnamon stick with the check mark is closest to you, it signals a positive outcome. If the cinnamon stick with the "X," is closest to you, it signals a negative outcome. If the blank cinnamon stick is nearest to you, the outcome is not yet determined and you can do a working to draw abundance to you.

SPELL FOR A SPECIFIC SUM OF MONEY

When an unexpected expense, need, or desire arises, I rely on this simple cinnamon spell. Cinnamon is renowned for attracting abundance, and fire energy is all about swift action. Consider using Abundance & Blessings Oil (page 114) to enhance your money-drawing efforts, although any anointing liquid will suffice. It's important to sprinkle these magick-infused ashes into your left shoe, which is the receiving side, to bring money directly to you.

Materials

Pen and paper
Anointing liquid
Ground cinnamon
Tweezers or small tongs
Match or lighter
Fireproof vessel

Instructions

1. Write the sum of money that you need on the paper, then anoint the four corners.

2. Fold the paper in half toward you and sprinkle some ground cinnamon inside. Then fold the paper in half again toward you.

3. Using the tweezers or tongs to hold the paper, light it and hold it over the fireproof vessel while watching it burn. As you do this, bring your focused attention to the energy in the flames. Feel the warmth feeding the attraction magick, bringing the money to you. Focus on the feeling of already having it.

4. After the paper has burned completely, collect the ashes. Choose a pair of shoes that you wear regularly and sprinkle the ashes into your left shoe.

5. Repeat this spell weekly until you receive the money you are seeking.

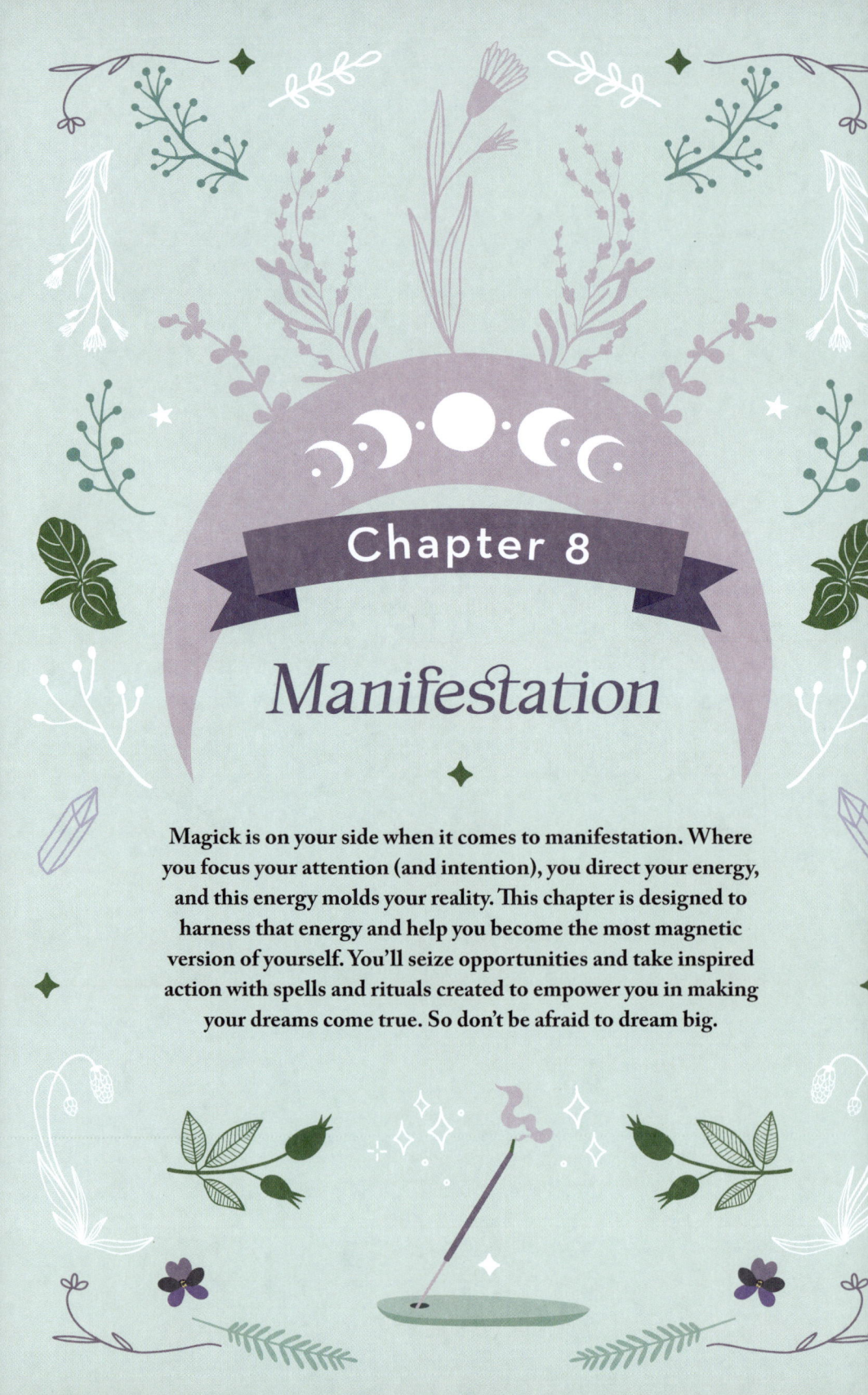

Chapter 8

Manifestation

Magick is on your side when it comes to manifestation. Where you focus your attention (and intention), you direct your energy, and this energy molds your reality. This chapter is designed to harness that energy and help you become the most magnetic version of yourself. You'll seize opportunities and take inspired action with spells and rituals created to empower you in making your dreams come true. So don't be afraid to dream big.

NEW MOON MANIFESTATION RITUAL FOR SETTING GOALS

At the start of the cycle, the new moon symbolizes beginnings, making it the perfect time to set goals and intentions. The lunar energy is strongest the day before, the day of, and the day after its peak. A white candle serves as a connection to the moon, but you can boost a specific manifestation by swapping it out for a color that aligns with your goal. (See Correspondences & Substitutions on page 211.) Bay leaf, the queen of manifestation materials, plays a classic role in this ritual. In the end, you'll use earth energy for steady progress by sprinkling ashes at the base of a tree or a potted plant.

Materials

White candle

Dried bay leaves

Permanent marker

Tweezers or small tongs

Fireproof vessel

Journal

→⫸ Instructions ⫷←

1. On the night of the new moon, light the candle.

2. Use the marker to draw a sigil that represents your goal on a dried bay leaf. You can use multiple bay leaves to manifest different goals, but only one sigil and goal per bay leaf.

3. One at a time, hold a bay leaf with the tweezers or small tongs, carefully light it from the candle's flame, and say:

   "From fire and ash,

   you manifest fast."

4. After you've burned all of your bay leaves, sprinkle the ashes at the base of a living tree as you say:

   "From seed to tree,

   and so it is, I decree."

More Manifestation Magick

Follow this ritual up with the Full Moon Ritual for Self-Reflection & Gratitude (page 131) to continue the magickal cycle and aid in your manifestations.

BLESSINGS ABOUND GRATITUDE RITUAL

Gratitude is the cornerstone of any spiritual practice. If you aim to facilitate positive manifestations, expressing gratitude helps you attune your energy to that of abundance. In this ritual, a white or gold candle symbolizes brilliant, overflowing abundance all around you. Olive oil, renowned for centuries as a sacred substance, represents fruitful rewards. Wild cherries bring passion, and basil beckons good fortune.

Materials

Items that represent what you are grateful for

Sewing pin or other sharp object for etching

White or gold candle

Olive oil

Dried basil, rosemary, and
wild cherry blossoms or bark

Small plate or saucer

⤳⧵ *Instructions* ⧸⧸⧼

1. Sit quietly in a comfortable place and take a few deep breaths. Place the items that represent what you are grateful for out before you or on an altar. Use the pin to etch the word "gratitude" into the side of the candle.

2. Add a few drops of the olive oil to your fingers and anoint the candle, moving from the top to the bottom toward you, being careful not to coat the wick.

3. Sprinkle a little bit of the basil, rosemary, and wild cherry on your working surface and roll the candle into the herbs.

4. Place the candle on a small plate or saucer before adding the rest of the herbs to the plate.

5. Light the candle and gaze into the flame. Let it fill your heart with warmth and joy as you think of the things you are grateful for. Say:

   "From within my heart,

   where blessings are found,

   gratitude is felt, love abounds."

6. Use your fingers and another few drops of olive oil to anoint each item that you placed before you.

7. Anoint your heart, then place your hands over your heart and say:

   "In body, mind, and spirit,

   I declare my gratitude

   so the Universe can hear it."

8. Spend some time here in meditation, receiving any messages that come to you. Allow the candle to burn all the way down or respectfully extinguish it and relight it consecutively with the same intention until it is finished.

FULL MOON RITUAL FOR SELF-REFLECTION & GRATITUDE

The full moon signifies the peak of your intentions and goals set during the new moon. It's a time of culmination. Using it to express gratitude for your progress and reflect on your actions and desires can help you let go of what no longer serves you and make room for new and better manifestations. In this ritual, a white candle amplifies your magick with lunar energy, and dried sage imparts wisdom. Select your favorite incense or consider using Manifesting Magick Incense (page 132). Once you've enchanted the key, keep it on your altar or in a special place to symbolize how your magick is unlocking doors.

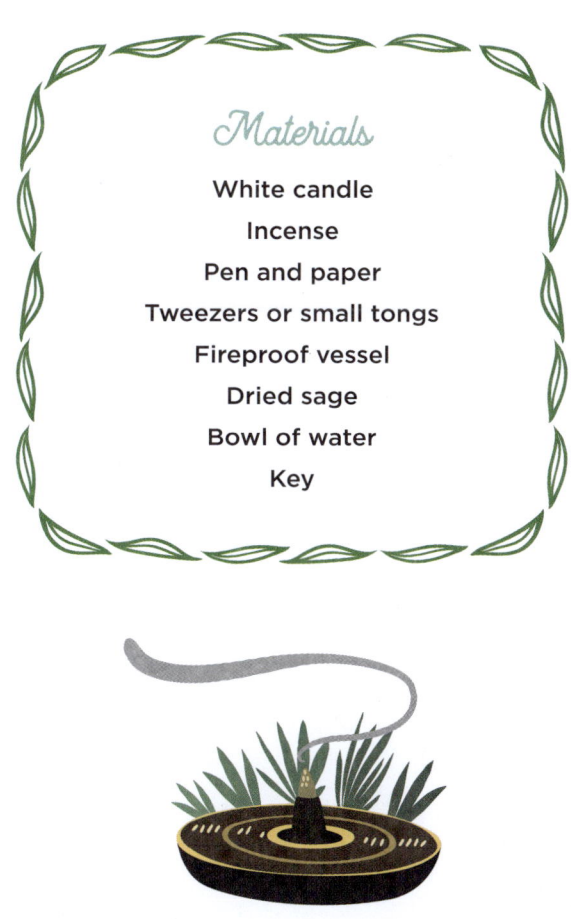

Materials

White candle

Incense

Pen and paper

Tweezers or small tongs

Fireproof vessel

Dried sage

Bowl of water

Key

1. Light the white candle and incense. Take a few moments to meditate on the manifestations and intentions you set during the new moon.

2. Separate a piece of paper into two columns. At the top of one column, write "I release." In that column, list the things that you feel have been standing in your way or have posed a challenge in your journey to achieving your goals. If you haven't encountered any challenges, then leave this side blank.

3. On top of the second column, write "I am grateful for." In this column, write down what you are grateful for in your journey toward achieving your goals.

4. Hold this paper with the tweezers or tongs, carefully light it from the white candle's flame, and hold it over the fireproof vessel. As it burns, say:

    "Wisdom gained from what's received,

    I release what's no longer needed."

5. Allow it to burn completely to ash, then sprinkle the dried sage over the ashes and mix them together. Sprinkle the mixture into the bowl of water.

6. Drop the key into the bowl of water and say:

    "Thank you for the blessings bestowed.

    I've removed all blocks and opened this road."

7. Leave the bowl out under the full moon or beside a window to allow the Universe to align with your intentions. The next morning, pour the water out in a natural setting.

Manifesting Magick Incense

Enhance any manifestation with this spiritually captivating incense blend. In a mortar and pestle or an electric coffee grinder, blend dried bay leaves, calendula, coriander, jasmine, mullein, and powdered pine gum until you have a fragrance you like and a fine powder equaling about ½ cup. Mix into that 2½ tablespoons of makko powder, a drizzle of honey, and a few drops of water until you have a workable paste. Shape the paste into cones or sticks and allow them to dry completely before burning them as incense.

A POPPET TO DOUBLE YOUR EFFORTS

Enhance your magickal manifestation power by crafting a clay poppet as your personal representation. This little doll acts as your magickal assistant, amplifying your efforts and maintaining your connection to the physical realm through sympathetic magick. By incorporating borage into the clay, you strengthen the metaphysical link. A personal item, like a strand of hair, connects your magickal and physical selves.

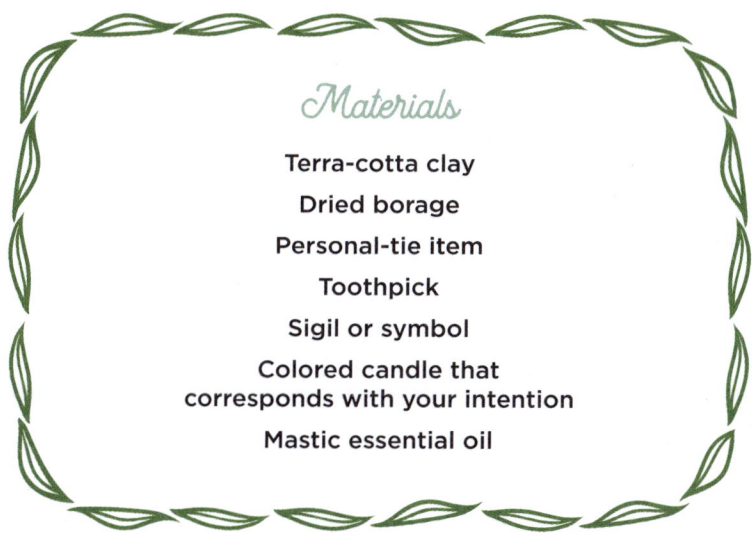

Materials

Terra-cotta clay

Dried borage

Personal-tie item

Toothpick

Sigil or symbol

Colored candle that corresponds with your intention

Mastic essential oil

⤜≫⤛ Instructions ⤜≪⤛

1. Set a very clear purpose for your poppet before you begin. This will help define the role of your magickal attendant and how you want it to help you.

2. Take the clay and knead the dried borage into it. Place your personal-tie item in what will be the center of your poppet before you begin to form a shape that represents you—whether a traditional human-like form or another shape that you identify with.

3. Mold your clay into your desired shape. Concentrate on your particular goal and imbue the poppet with your focused intention, emotions, and energy as it takes shape. This will give your likeness a sense of purpose.

4. Once you are happy with your sculpture, use the toothpick to draw a sigil or symbol in the clay that connects your poppet with your focused intention and its purpose.

5. Let your clay harden according to the manufacturer's instructions. Once it is dry, place the poppet on your altar and light the candle.

6. To activate your magick, drop 1 to 3 drops of mastic essential oil over your poppet as you communicate once more your specific purpose and focused intention.

7. Let the candle burn for a time that feels right to you. Then respectfully extinguish the candle.

8. Return daily, or as often as possible, to relight the candle for a few moments and add more mastic essential oil to your poppet until your purpose is fulfilled.

CLOVERLEAF TAROT MANIFESTATION SPELL

It's no secret that clovers are thought to bring good luck. This spell utilizes this serendipitous symbol, along with a Tarot deck and your own intuition, to help you manifest exactly what is meant for you. Your Tarot card's purpose is to sympathetically attract what you need, but interpreting the card sometimes offers additional clarity as well. You can use any liquid for anointing, though I love Abundance & Blessings Oil (page 114) for this. Flip to the Correspondences & Substitutions section (page 211) to choose a candle color that best suits your goal. (For help interpreting your Tarot card, you can turn to page 216 for further clarity.)

Materials

Tarot deck

Dried red clover

Anointing liquid

Candle in a color that corresponds with your intention

Pen and paper

Paper clip

➤➤➤ Instructions ❮❮❮

1. Begin by separating the cards, setting aside the major arcana. Determine which suit aligns with your desired manifestation:

   a. Wands for desires and passions

   b. Cups for emotions and intuition

   c. Swords for ideas, creativity, knowledge, and boundaries

   d. Pentacles for money, material matters, stability, and health

2. Create a pile with all the cards from the suit that matches your goal. Shuffle these cards while asking for guidance on the necessary steps to reach your goal.

3. Draw one card and place it on your working surface. This card can offer additional insight into your situation.

4. Anoint the candle with the anointing liquid, avoiding the wick, and roll it in the dried clover. Light the candle and position it on top of the Tarot card.

5. Let the candle burn completely or respectfully extinguish it and relight it consecutively with the same intention until it is finished.

6. Using the paper and pen, draw a customized sigil (see page 17), and secure it to the Tarot card with a paperclip. Keep it on your altar or under your pillow for one month.

Symbols of Luck, Protection, and Fairy Sight

In folklore, four-leaf clovers have the power to grant the holder good luck, ward off evil spirits, and give you the ability to see fairies. Only 1 in 10,000 clovers has four leaves, making finding one a rare and lucky event.

MANIFESTATION PAPER SPELL

Performing a paper spell is a great way to articulate your desires and intentions, leaving no room for confusion. This comes in handy because, when you're working with energy to fulfill your goals, it's important to be explicit and clear about your purpose to avoid unintended consequences. Be mindful not to box yourself in. However, I do suggest adding a line of protection into your paper spell, such as "with harm to none" or "if it serves my higher purpose."

In your paper spell, you can address a specific spirit (such as a god, ancestors, or guides) or the Universe as a whole. The act of creating your request may stand as a spell in itself, but you can also combine it with other objects as part of a larger spell. For a bit of added magick, use Green Witch's Spell Paper to Attain Your Wishes (page 138) and Money Magnet Ink (page 121) or Passion Pigment Ink (page 161).

Materials

Pen and paper

Instructions

1. Begin by writing about your gratitude for the opportunities and blessings that you've received thus far.

2. Move on to what you hope to manifest, writing your charm in the present tense as if you've already received your desires. Be specific about what you are seeking and how you will feel once you've received it, giving as much detail as possible. Make sure you focus on what you *do* want instead of what you *don't* want. For example, instead of writing "I don't want to be in debt," write "I am abundantly wealthy." You can include a set time frame, but I encourage you to be open to divine timing.

3. End the spell with an offering—such as a small cup of wine or juice, an herb or flower, or a song—to strengthen your request. Simply place the offering on top of or beside your paper spell.

4. Keep the paper on your altar or in another safe place. You can feed this spell, either monthly or anytime you feel the need, using the methods mentioned in Energize Your Spells: Fueling Your Magick (page 147).

Green Witch's Spell Paper to Attain Your Wishes

You can use this magick-infused paper for any spell, but it's particularly good for your Manifestation Paper Spell (page 137). Set out pieces of paper in a single layer on a rimmed baking dish. Bring a pot of water to a boil, then turn off the heat and add 3 tablespoons of black tea to strengthen your magick, a pinch of turmeric for protection, a pinch of lavender for luck, and a pinch of chamomile for wishes. Steep the ingredients for 15 minutes, then strain the solids from the mixture and carefully pour the liquid over the baking sheet to cover the paper. Let the pieces of paper soak overnight. Then carefully remove them from the water and lay them flat to dry.

Bay Leaf Enchantments for Enhancing Manifestations

Bay leaf is a versatile magickal ingredient that is great for beginner witches. It symbolizes victory, which is why it is so efficient at amplifying energy. Here are a few ways you can use it:

- Fuel the energy of your manifestations by placing a bay leaf in your journal or incorporating one into your vision board.

- Place a bay leaf inside your day planner to ensure you cross everything off your to-do list.

- Carry a bay leaf in your purse or wallet to attract money.

- Add a bay leaf to your tea and stir it clockwise while reciting your affirmations and focused intentions.

BOX OF DESIRES MANIFESTATION SPELL

This manifestation spell is ready for you to make it your own. You can use any type of box with a lid—for example, a shoe box, a jewelry box, or a gift box. Any anointing liquid will work, but I like to use Oil of Purposeful Action (page 146) or Goal-Getter Solar Water (page 144) when manifesting. You'll add herbs and minerals that support your specific goals. (Check out Correspondences & Substitutions on page 211 for ideas.) You can also decorate the box with colors, sigils, and other items that align with your intentions.

Materials

Box with lid

Decorations that support your intentions (optional)

Desire Drawing Dust (page 140) or Green Grains of Plenty (page 122)

Pen and paper

Dried bay leaf

Herbs and crystals that support your intention

Anointing liquid

Magick Is What You Make It

You might be surprised by the different kinds of containers you can use for magick. Cauldrons, cups, bottles, bags, and boxes are among my favorite vessels. Essentially, whatever you have on hand will do if you infuse it with your intention.

❯❯❯ Instructions ❮❮❮

1. Decorate your box any way you like.

2. Add a layer of Desire Drawing Dust or Green Grains of Plenty to the bottom of the box.

3. Write a detailed paper spell, stating exactly what you want as if you already have it and how you will feel once you've received it. Then fold it toward you and place the bay leaf inside.

4. Add the petition to the box along with any herbs and crystals that you've chosen.

5. Put the lid on the box. Use the anointing liquid to draw a clockwise spiral on the top while saying:

    "My wildest dreams are unlocked

    within this manifestation box."

6. Be sure to feed and charge your manifestation box regularly using the methods in Energize Your Spells: Fueling Your Magick (page 147).

Desire Drawing Dust

This blend of plant allies is well known for granting wishes. To bring your desires to fruition, create a manifestation powder by grinding dried bay leaf, cardamom, cinnamon, dandelion, rose petals, and sunflower petals into a fine powder using a mortar and pestle or an electric coffee grinder. Store the powder with hematite and tiger's eye stones in a lidded container. With your hands over the container, focus your intention to charge the mixture with the energy needed to manifest your dreams.

SPELL CANDLES TO OBTAIN WHAT YOU SEEK

One day, as I was struggling to dress a spell candle, I thought, *What if you could dress them from the inside?* That's when I remembered one of the best crafts I learned as a child: how to make rolled beeswax candles. Beeswax candle sheets are thin and flexible and come in a variety of colors. When rolled, they create clean, fast-burning taper candles. And you can make them in any size you choose, which really comes in handy when you don't have time to wait for a spell candle to burn down completely. You can use the candles you make in any spell or ritual. Simply choose a wax color, an anointing liquid, and safe-to-burn herbs that align with your need or desire. (You can use the lists at the back of this book for ideas.)

Materials

Beeswax sheets

Anointing liquid

Herbs that correspond with your intention

Wicks made for rolled beeswax candles

Instructions

1. Cut your beeswax sheet into a rectangle of your desired size. (A 3 × 4-inch rectangle comes out to be about the same size as most chime candles.)

2. Hold the sheet between your hands to warm it and make it more pliable.

3. Use a drop or two of anointing liquid to draw onto the beeswax sheet any words or symbols that align with your intention. Or, if you prefer, simply anoint the sheet in any way that feels right to you, such as in the corners or in a spiral.

4. Sprinkle a small amount of your chosen herbs evenly over the beeswax sheet.

5. Place the wick along the long edge of the sheet, making sure that it extends 1½ inches beyond the top.

6. Fold the edge over the wick and gently press down to secure it. Then gently roll the sheet into a cylindrical candle. (If it starts to crack, warm the sheet using a hair dryer set to low.) Then roll the candle back and forth to seal and shape it.

7. Trim the wick to ¼ inch before burning.

Chapter 9

Luck
&
Success

It's no secret that people turn to all manner of charms to invite luck into their lives. People have believed in the influence of certain symbols and gestures—from horseshoes and clovers to ladybugs and elephants—to attract good fortune since ancient times. Over the centuries, these beliefs have evolved into a dance of serendipity and hard work. Natural magick can help you tip the scales. When you need an extra dose of luck, this chapter will teach you how to create your own. And if you encounter a streak of bad luck, rest assured that it can be broken.

SHILLING SPELL OF SUCCESS

A shilling or sixpence is considered a symbol of good luck, prosperity, and health (hence the tradition of placing a coin in a bride's shoe on her wedding day), which makes it the perfect centerpiece of this spell. You can easily find these coins online or in antique shops. But if you can't get a sixpence, a quarter or any silver coin will do. And basil and chamomile support prosperity in countless ways. For an added magickal boost, use Abundance & Blessings Oil (page 114) for anointing and perform this spell during the waxing moon, which symbolizes growth and increase.

Materials

Anointing liquid
Sixpence piece or other silver coin
Pouch, sachet, or cloth and string
Dried basil and chamomile

Instructions

1. Anoint the coin, place it in the pouch, then add the basil and chamomile.

2. Holding the pouch in your hands, whisper to it:

   "Savoring the sweetness of success,

   I stand in this moment truly blessed.

   With gratitude in my heart and a spirit that's free,

   I embrace the blessings that have come to me."

3. Place the pouch in a shoe you wear often for one day and one night (while you wear a different pair) before moving it to a space that aligns with your hard work, such as your office or altar.

GOAL-GETTER SOLAR WATER

The practice of making sun-blessed water is very similar to that of making moon-blessed water (page 36). Both are versatile assets for any practitioner. Charging water with the essence of the full sun infuses it with potent fire energy and the sun's radiant power, which offers energetic purification, protection, passion, and courage. The essential components are just water and a vessel; everything else aids your focused intention. I really love using this solar water as a spray to activate and energize myself and my magickal tools. If you want to give it a boost, add citrine and clear quartz chips followed by a few drops of glycerin or vitamin E oil to preserve it.

Materials

Large, clear bowl

2 cups orange-blossom water

Dried hazel, violet, or chicory

Cardamom, rosemary, and ylang-ylang essential oils

Jar with lid

Instructions

1. In the early morning, fill a cleansed bowl with 2 cups of orange-blossom water followed by a generous pinch of hazel, violet, or chicory.

2. Set the mixture out in a spot where it will remain in full sunlight for most of the day.

3. Once it is no longer in direct sunlight, strain the water into the jar and discard the solids.

4. Add the essential oils to the water, secure the lid of the jar, and shake your intention into the mixture. As you do this, say:

    "Blessed by the sun to empower action,

    with fire, drive, and magnetic attraction."

EFFICIENCY ENCHANTMENT FOR INSPIRED ACTION

This spell not only brings good luck but also primes you for swift action, thanks to the presence of ginger, which ensures you're ready to seize any opportunities that come your way. In addition, lemongrass helps you set clear goals and visualize your success, while carnelian provides energy for growth. To make this spell even more effective, try using Oil of Purposeful Action (page 146) as an anointing liquid.

Materials

Anointing liquid
Orange candle
Slice of fresh ginger
Dried lemongrass
Carnelian stone
Pouch or cloth with string

Instructions

1. Anoint the orange candle with the anointing liquid, moving toward yourself from the top to the base, then light it.

2. Anoint your forehead, eyes, mouth, heart, belly, hands, and feet.

3. Using the ginger like a wand, wave it over the same areas to charge them with active energy.

4. Place the lemongrass and carnelian in the pouch, then place the pouch in front of the candle to charge it with your focused intention.

5. Let the candle burn all the way down, or respectfully extinguish it and relight it consecutively with the same intention until it is finished.

6. Carry the pouch with you when you need to be productive, and sleep with it under your pillow when you need to be up bright and early to seize the day.

OIL OF PURPOSEFUL ACTION

There's nothing quite like solar energy to empower and ignite the flames of motivation and propel yourself forward. Perform this spell during the day, preferably while sitting outside or by a window. Even a cloudy day will work, though a sunny one is better. The sun will infuse the working and its materials with its energy. Sunflowers, a key ingredient, lend their upbeat nature to this potion. If you can't find them, dandelions or chamomile will also provide an uplifting presence. Thyme supplies plenty of courage, ginger and damiana provide passion, and mint offers protection. For even more radiant vibrations, use sunflower oil for the base—but olive oil is a great runner-up.

Materials

Pint jar with lid

Dried damiana, ginger, mint, and thyme

Fresh or dried sunflowers

Sunflower oil or olive oil

Citrine or clear quartz stone (optional)

Dropper bottles

Instructions

1. Take a few deep breaths and visualize a bright, sunny day. Feel the warmth and light of the sun above you, blessing you and charging you with solar energy.

2. Fill a cleansed jar with the dried damiana, ginger, mint, thyme, and sunflowers. As you do this, communicate your focused intention for purposeful action. If you have a specific goal in mind, think about the steps you will take to get there.

3. Pour the oil over the herbs, leaving just a small space at the top of the jar.

4. Secure the lid and shake in your intention.

5. Place your potion outside or in a sunny window to charge with solar energy for about an hour (even if it is a cloudy day).

6. Bring the jar inside and store it out of direct sunlight for 2 to 4 weeks with the citrine or quartz crystal (if you've chosen to use one) on top of the jar.

7. Once the mixture has fully steeped, strain it and discard the solids. Decant the oil into dropper bottles for easy use in spellwork.

Energize Your Spells: Fueling Your Magick

A spell is at its strongest when you release its energy into the Universe. However, over time, this energy naturally dissipates. That's why it's essential to continuously infuse, or feed, energy into your spells throughout the process. This ongoing practice is key to ensuring effective and long-lasting results.

Energizing your spells can be as simple as shaking an oil that you are infusing, adding more ingredients to a container spell, lighting a candle or incense with intention, setting your workings out under full moonlight or sunlight, or recharging them with your personal energy. To enhance your magick and raise its vibration, you can also chant over your spell. Whatever you do, instill within your spells sincere, focused intentions and strong emotions to channel your energy effectively and bring your desires to fruition.

Salt Water for Luck's Renewal

To banish a spell of bad luck, sprinkle three pinches of salt into a glass of water before going to bed. Stir the water three times counterclockwise with your finger. Then, using the same finger, tap the edge of the glass three times. Dip your finger into the salt water and draw a crescent moon on your forehead before placing the glass on your bedside table to work as you sleep. When you awaken in the morning, pour the water down the drain along with your bad luck.

CHAOS SHIELD FOR MERCURY RETROGRADE

When it's that time of year again, I use this energetic shield to protect me from Mercury's mischief. Salt and sage are classic ingredients that will shield you, while lavender offers peace, lemon balm brings success, and yarrow enhances communication. For more energetic oomph, you can add minerals like amazonite, hematite, or smokey quartz. Perform this spell the night before Mercury retrograde.

Materials

Bowl or jar

Salt

Dried lavender, lemon balm, sage, and yarrow

Personal-tie item

Washable marker

Crystals aligned with intentions (optional)

Instructions

1. To a cleansed bowl or jar, add the salt, sage, lavender, lemon balm, and yarrow.

2. Stir the ingredients counterclockwise three times, then draw the Mercury (☿) symbol in the mixture with your finger and place your personal-tie item in the middle.

3. If you have chosen to add any crystals, do so now.

4. Set the bowl outside any door in your home or by a window.

5. Using the washable marker, draw the Mercury (☿) symbol on your palm before going to bed.

6. When you awaken the next morning, immediately wash your hands to remove the ink.

7. Keep the bowl out until Mercury has gone direct, at which point you should discard the salt mixture in the outside trash bin and cleanse the other items.

Simple Charm Bag for Good Luck

Carrying a talisman charmed to bring you good luck is a simple act of magick that unites us all. Instead of carrying a lucky rabbit's foot, though, try a simple pouch filled with Rose of Jericho to resurrect old luck, heather to draw in new luck, lemon balm for success, cloves for protection, and orange to attract good fortune. Hold the bag or bundle in your hands and charge it with your energy, being sure to regularly fuel it with your focused intention.

The Luck of Three Charm Braid for Wellness, Happiness, and Prosperity

Within this braid, each of the three parts symbolizes a distinct intention—wellness, happiness, and prosperity—that you want to weave into your life. Select a ¼- to ½-inch section from an inconspicuous area and divide it into three parts. Apply Botanical Shielding Oil (page 57) and then braid the sections, focusing on wellness, happiness, and prosperity. (If your hair is too short to braid, you can use the oil to draw three interwoven circles on a hair accessory, like a barrette, with the same intentions.) Enhance the braid's magick by adding colored embroidery floss or charms matching your intentions. Alternatively, you can braid cord together with a few strands of your hair and wear it as a bracelet with the same magickal properties.

HORSESHOE GOOD-LUCK CHARM

The first thing I hang up over the door in a new home is a broom. The second is this horseshoe charm. Horseshoes, traditionally made of iron, are believed to ward off bad luck and negativity. Adding copper wire as a conduit for energy can enhance your magick and amplify the purpose of your chosen pendant that represents good luck to you. Just make sure to hang your horseshoe open side up to capture and hold good luck, as hanging it upside down may let the luck spill out.

Materials

Candle

Relaxing music

Horseshoe

Copper jewelry wire

Pendant

Oil of Purposeful Action (page 146)
or other anointing liquid

Instructions

1. Find a comfortable place to sit, light a candle, and put on some relaxing music.

2. Holding the horseshoe with the ends pointing upward, push a 10-inch piece of copper wire through the top hole in one side. Wrap the wire around that side of the horseshoe to secure it.

3. Hang the pendant on the copper wire, then bring the wire through the top hole on the other side, wrapping it to secure it. (It should look like your horseshoe is wearing a necklace.)

4. When you're ready, use the anointing liquid to bless the horseshoe while saying:
   "Opportunities unfold, as far as the eye can see.
   Good luck now flows abundantly to me."

5. Hang the horseshoe over your primary entrance or bedroom door.

Simple Charms for Blessing Others

What we put out into the Universe, we receive back. Blessing others is a way to keep the positive energy flowing. To do this, whisper a blessing to a small object, such as a crystal, stone, or coin. Then place it where someone else will discover it, passing the blessings on to the finder. Here's a list of possible blessings, but you can also create your own:

- I hope that you always feel loved and valued.

- Sending you courage, strength, and grace in times of challenge.

- Wishing you love and laughter throughout your life.

- May peace, serenity, and health surround you always.

- Sending you good vibes, positive energy, and a life of abundance.

- May your path be lined with abundance, success, and fulfillment.

- May your heart be at ease, your spirit be free, and forever blessings be.

- Wishing that you have moments of pure contentment and days filled with joy.

- May you be surrounded by friends and family who love and support you always.

- May you find joy in the small things.

- Sending you heartfelt wishes for a wonderful day.

- May each step bring you closer to your dreams.

- May you have an abundant life filled with promise.

- May your path be filled with kindness and magick.

- Wishing you good health, wisdom, and prosperity.

- Blessings for a boundless heart.

- Sending you positive energy of fulfillment and purpose.

Chapter 10

Love & Passion

Who doesn't desire connection and companionship?
Whether we admit it or not, we are social creatures,
seeking meaningful connections with others. This
chapter is full of spells and charms to help you
find love, passion, and romance. But should you
find yourself in need of repelling an unwanted
lover, well, there's a spell for that too, my dear.

BLOOMING HEART BEADS TO DRAW LOVE

Made using fresh rose petals, these beads keep you consistently in tune with loving vibrations. Pink, peach, or classic red roses are best, as they keep a lovely color even after they've dried. The beads are brilliant on their own, but adding essential oil can enhance their qualities. The key, a symbol of opening, aids in unlocking the love that's right for you. Get creative and use other items for decoration, such as feathers, crystals, and trinkets.

Materials

Blender or food processor

Petals of 6 fresh roses (about 2 cups)

1 teaspoon ground cinnamon

Silicone spatula

Paper towels

Toothpicks

Food dehydrator or microwave

String or cord

Key

Any combination of the following essential oils: lavender, jasmine, neroli, patchouli, rose, ylang-ylang

⇥⇥ *Instructions* ⇤⇤

1. To a blender or food processor, add the fresh rose petals and ground cinnamon, then blend until broken down, using a spatula to scrape down the sides as needed. You may need to add a few drops of water to get the mixture going, but do so sparingly. When finished, the mixture should resemble about ¼ cup of wet sand and hold its shape when pressed.

2. Turn the mixture out onto paper towels. Squeeze and compress about a teaspoon of the rose petal mixture into a ball around the middle of a toothpick to create a hole for threading. Keep squeezing, releasing water as you do so, until the bead is the desired shape. (Keep in mind, it's likely to become a rough round shape and not a perfect ball.)

3. Continue creating beads until you have at least six; you can make more if you like. Freeze any remaining mixture for another time.

4. Place the beads in a food dehydrator for a few hours, in a microwave at 30-second intervals, or out in the sun for a few days until completely dry.

5. When dry, gently pull out the toothpicks, then string the beads and the key into a garland, tassel, jewelry, or other aesthetically pleasing design.

6. Add a few drops of the essential oils to the beads. Then, holding the string in your hands, enchant them with your desire by saying:

    "With open hearts and spirits aligned,

    my true love and I are intertwined.

    An opened path, holding the key,

    I attract the right one for me."

ROMANCE RICE FOR PASSION

Craft this harmonious medley to help you manifest the romance, love, and connection you desire. The base ingredient—grain—symbolizes growth, nourishment, and unity. Geraniums are known for their loving, passionate, and romantic energy and are often used to attract or strengthen a relationship. And the color red has long represented romantic love and good luck. In this recipe, that color comes from dragon fruit, which will protect and amplify your magick, or beetroot, which symbolizes love and beauty. But if you don't have either on hand, a few drops of red food coloring will do. Use this rice in love spells or in the Cauldron of Desire Ritual (page 157).

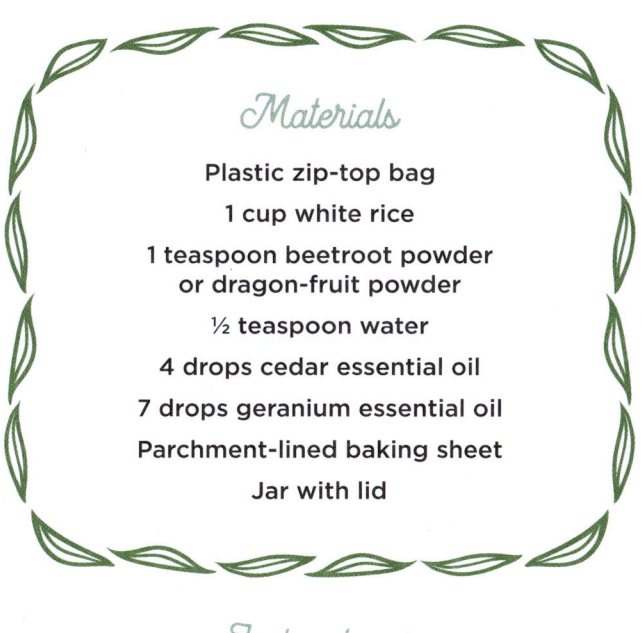

Materials

Plastic zip-top bag

1 cup white rice

1 teaspoon beetroot powder
or dragon-fruit powder

½ teaspoon water

4 drops cedar essential oil

7 drops geranium essential oil

Parchment-lined baking sheet

Jar with lid

Instructions

1. To a plastic zip-top bag, add the rice, beetroot or dragon-fruit powder, water, and essential oils.

2. Close the bag tight, then shake it to incorporate the mixture.

3. When it's well incorporated, open the bag and spread the mixture onto a parchment-lined baking sheet.

4. Set the baking sheet out in the sun to charge the mixture with fire energy until it is completely dry. Store the rice in a lidded jar.

Charms for Finding the Right Person

Even the smallest practices hold the power to invoke love magick. Attracting the right person could be as simple as:

- Painting sigils and symbols on your nails and using Oil of Allure (page 162) as cuticle oil daily.

- Keeping a bottle of Amour Essence Powder (page 159) or Romance Rice (page 155) with you.

- Arranging a bouquet of yarrow and roses to enhance your romantic intuition.

- Sleeping with mugwort and lavender under your pillow and asking to dream of your future love.

- Taking a bath in jasmine and neroli oil.

- Making and wearing a necklace made of rose hips.

- Enjoying a cup of tea made with rose and marshmallow.

Ritual to Revive Your Relationship

Do you need to rekindle the flames of passion and romance in your relationship? Start with the Romance Rice recipe, but instead of using regular water, use water from a Rose of Jericho plant, also known as the "resurrection plant." (You can also buy this bottled.) Then fill a glass jar or vial halfway with Romance Rice, clear quartz chips, and rose quartz chips. Seal the jar and give it a gentle shake whenever you need to ignite romance and passion. You can also give a vial to your partner and ask them to do the same.

CAULDRON OF DESIRE RITUAL TO DRAW LOVE INTO YOUR LIFE

Every day of the week offers an opportunity for creating more powerful magick. Friday is governed by Venus, known for its grace, charisma, sensuality, and sociability. It's also associated with Freja, the Norse goddess of passionate love, and Frigg, who is associated with love and marriage. Performing this ritual on a Friday will supercharge it with the magnetic energy of love, drawing more to you. You can use any bowl or cauldron, but don't forget the apple seeds—they are the energetic focal point of this ritual. And gold brings the action by infusing your magick with solar essence.

Materials

3 fresh roses, red or pink

Romance Rice (page 155)

Bowl

Gold permanent marker or paint pen

Apple seeds

Dried rosemary

⇝⇝ Instructions ⇜⇜

1. On a Friday, hold the three roses up to your heart while immersing yourself in the sensations and emotions associated with love. Imagine a warm, radiant light and a feeling of deep affection and connection.

2. Pull the petals off of one rose while saying:

   "Deep within my heart, I know that I am deserving of love."

3. Remove the petals from the second rose as you say:

   "I attract the love that is worthy of me."

4. As you remove the petals from the third rose, say:

   "Like a magnet, I draw love's energy into my life."

5. Add a base layer of Romance Rice to the bowl.

6. On a few rose petals, use the marker to write down all of the attributes that you are looking for in a partner (one attribute per petal).

7. Place all of the rose petals, including the ones you've written on, in the bowl. Then sprinkle the apple seeds and rosemary into the bowl.

8. Place the bowl on your altar or in another energetically charged place. Continue to imbue it with your energy while saying the previous three incantations over the course of days or weeks until you feel it's done its job. (Feel free to use your hands to stir your intention into the mixture.)

AMOUR ESSENCE POWDER TO ATTRACT LOVE

It won't take much of this enchanting and aromatic botanical blend to beckon love into your life. With catnip to draw love toward you, rose for passion, jasmine for desire, lavender for love, and hibiscus for joy, you'll open a pathway of ever-flowing affection and adoration. And we can't forget a touch of cinnamon to quicken your magick and a bit of arrowroot to ground it. (Just a pinch can work wonders!) For best results, let this mixture charge under the full moon.

Materials

Mortar and pestle or electric coffee grinder

2 tablespoons dried catnip

2 tablespoons orris root

2 tablespoons damiana

2 tablespoons dried hibiscus

2 tablespoons dried jasmine

2 tablespoons dried lavender

2 tablespoons dried rose petals

Jar with lid

1 teaspoon ground cinnamon

4 tablespoons arrowroot powder

7 drops geranium or jasmine essential oil

Rose quartz stone

→≫+ Instructions +≪←

1. Using the mortar and pestle or electric coffee grinder, grind the catnip, orris root, damiana, hibiscus, jasmine, lavender, and rose petals until you have a fine powder.

2. Pour the mixture into the jar and add the ground cinnamon, arrowroot powder, and essential oil.

3. Secure the lid and shake your focused intention into the jar.

4. Close your eyes and envision a pink beam of light forming a path before you. Sense love's energy drawing toward you; feel your magnetic attraction to it and it to you.

5. Add the rose quartz to the jar, then charge the entire container under the next full moon.

Uses for Amour Essence Powder

Amour Essence Powder—how can I use thee? Let me count the ways:

- Dust a small amount of powder across your collarbone or clothing while focusing your intentions on the qualities you desire in a partner.

- Sprinkle the powder around your home, particularly in areas where you spend significant time, and envision moments with a future partner.

- Dip your finger in moon or sun water, then in the powder, and draw sigils and symbols on your primary door to welcome a lover's arrival.

- Use the powder to dress candles for love and attraction in spells.

- Scatter it across your path to beckon love to cross your journey.

- Place some of the powder in a pouch with rose quartz and carnelian and position it near your phone to encourage a lover to call.

PASSION PIGMENT INK

The perfect companion to passionate paper spells and love letters alike, this ink is full of sensual energy. Regardless of whether you choose raspberries, strawberries, or cherries, these red fruits are imbued with amorous love and desire. Damiana ignites feelings, honey adds sweetness, and rose water enhances the efficacy of your love spells.

Materials

½ cup rose water or regular water

1 cup fresh red berries or cherries

1 teaspoon dried damiana

Potato masher or fork

Cheesecloth

½ teaspoon honey

Airtight container

Instructions

1. Add the rose water, damiana, and fresh fruit to a pot and bring it to boil for 10 minutes. Then remove it from the heat and mash the contents using a potato masher or fork.

2. Strain the mixture through the cheesecloth and mix in the honey.

3. Pour the ink into an airtight storage container, leaving the lid off until it has cooled completely and thickened. Then secure the lid and store the ink in the refrigerator.

4. To use this ink, dip the tip of a feather, quill, twig, paintbrush, or pen in it and inscribe your incantations on the desired paper.

OIL OF ALLURE GLAMOUR FOR POSITIVE ATTENTION

Glamour magick is about enhancing the way others perceive you, not about physical transformation. It's helpful not only in love workings but also in job interviews, during a performance, and in self-love rituals. This glamour oil helps you create an instantly captivating aura. Cardamom enhances attraction, damiana fosters confidence, black pepper safeguards your intentions, and ylang-ylang and neroli infuse harmony. Lastly, the inviting fragrance of vanilla, associated with sensuality and passion, serves to sweeten any partnership.

Materials

Pint jar

5 cardamom pods

4 tablespoons dried damiana

4 tablespoons dried violet

Apricot or avocado oil

10 drops vanilla botanical extract

5 drops black pepper essential oil

5 drops ylang-ylang essential oil

5 drops neroli essential oil

Dropper bottles (optional)

Instructions

1. Fill the pint jar with the cardamom pods, damiana, and violet.

2. Add the apricot or avocado oil so that the other ingredients are completely covered.

3. Holding the jar in your hands, visualize a path unfolding before you that radiates positive energy. Feel anything that you desire coming toward you.

4. Allow the mixture to steep in a cool dark place for 2 to 4 weeks.

5. Strain the solids and discard them. Add to the remaining liquid the vanilla botanical extract, and the black pepper, ylang-ylang, and neroli essential oils.

6. Decant the oil into individual dropper bottles, if desired.

Green Witch's Spell Paper to Attain Your True Love

This simple, intention-infused paper can deepen any love spell. Set out pieces of paper on a rimmed baking dish. Bring a pot of water to a boil, then turn off the heat and add 3 tablespoons of white tea to protect your intention, a pinch of hibiscus for attraction, a few rose petals for love, a pinch of lavender for peace, and a pinch of chamomile for beauty. Steep the ingredients for 15 minutes, then strain the solids from the mixture and carefully pour the liquid over the baking sheet to cover the paper. Let the pieces of paper soak overnight, then carefully remove them from the water and lay them flat to dry. Use this paper in combination with the Passion Pigment Ink (page 161) for a potent punch of love magick.

Evergreen Love Incense for Eternal Attraction

When you want your magick to have staying power, make this earthy incense for longevity and a strong bond. With an electric coffee grinder or mortar and pestle, grind dried damiana, juniper, powdered pine gum, sage, and vetiver root into a fine powder until you have a fragrance you like and about ½ cup of the mixture. To that, add 2½ tablespoons of makko powder, a drizzle of honey, and a few drops of water until you have a workable paste. Shape this into cones or sticks and let them dry completely before burning.

Repel an Unwanted Admirer

When you want to keep someone at arm's length (or farther), work this simple charm. First, you'll need something that represents your unwanted admirer, such as a photo or a name or description written on paper. Put a few drops of Repulsion Oil to Banish Love (page 164) or Botanical Shielding Oil (page 57) on your finger and use it to draw an X over the item. Fill a lidded container with salt, then place the photo or paper face down in the salt. Secure the lid and store the container in your garage, shed, storage closet, or any other place that you do not visit frequently.

REPULSION OIL TO BANISH LOVE

The opposite of attraction magick, repulsion magick helps you keep something or someone at a distance. If you find yourself receiving uninvited affection, use this oil blend—which includes ingredients renowned for breaking love magick—as a deterrent. Anoint yourself or the objects you use in spells.

Materials

2-ounce dropper bottle

Castor oil

6 drops lily essential oil

6 drops lotus essential oil

6 drops black pepper essential oil

Obsidian chips (optional)

Instructions

1. Fill a dropper bottle with castor oil, leaving a small amount of space at the top.

2. Add the essential oils and a few obsidian chips, if desired.

3. Secure the lid, then shake your intention into the bottle.

4. Hold the bottle in your hands and charge it with your energy by thinking of things that repel or create barriers around you.

UNCASTING RITUAL TO REVERSE THE EFFECTS OF LOVE

Perhaps you have an unwanted admirer, or maybe you've cast a love spell and regret it. I'm not here to ask questions; I'm here to provide magickal solutions. Grab yourself some natural-fiber cord for knot magick, used to symbolically untie the bond.

Materials

Cotton, hemp, or other natural-fiber cord

Tweezers or small tongs

Match or lighter

Fireproof vessel

Black pepper

Salt

Cone incense

Instructions

1. First, tie three knots into the cord while saying:

   "In past and present, we were once bound."

2. Then untie all three knots while saying:

   "Now, in all realities, no love or bond is found."

3. Hold the cord with tweezers or tongs, light it, and let it burn in the fireproof vessel.

4. To the fireproof vessel, add the black pepper and salt. Then place the cone incense in the middle and light it.

5. Rub your hands through the smoke as if washing them, then use your hands to direct the smoke over your body while visualizing a waterfall washing over you.

6. Once the cone has burned down, mix it in with the salt and herbs to make a powder. Sprinkle this on the threshold of your doors and windows. Refresh the spell every Saturday as needed.

Chapter 11

♥

Relationships

We live in a world of relationships—some we come upon by chance, some we choose, and some relationships choose us. It is said that through these relationships, we experience our existence. When these connections are healthy and well maintained, the energy exchanged between individuals is mutually beneficial. Likewise, if it is an unhealthy interaction, it's not doing your energy any favors. From romantic partnerships that give you butterflies to enduring friendships that withstand the test of time, the spells in this section take your magick to a place where bonds are nurtured and souls find their kindred spirits.

SELF-LOVE RITUAL FOR RECLAIMING YOUR RADIANCE

Your most important relationship is the one you have with yourself. If you want to feel more confident and beautiful, then you'll need to see yourself as just that. This spell has what you need, with hibiscus for attraction, chamomile for beauty, lavender for luck, rose for love, and rice for abundant blessings. Castor oil and apricot oil equally share the spotlight in helping you to step into your magnificence.

Materials

Mortar and pestle or electric coffee grinder

Dried chamomile, hibiscus flower, lavender, and rose petals

Jar with lid

Rice powder

Castor and apricot oils

Mirror

Instructions

1. In a mortar and pestle or electric coffee grinder, blend the chamomile, hibiscus flower, lavender, and rose petals into a fine powder.

2. Pour the mixture into the jar and stir in the rice powder.

3. Add the castor and apricot oils to the blend and stir again.

4. Scoop out a quarter-sized amount of the mixture and use it to wash your face and hands.

5. Rinse it off, then gaze into a mirror while saying:

   "Mirror, mirror, I can see

   the beauty that's within me.

   Mirror, mirror, now it's time

   for everyone to see this beauty of mine."

6. Repeat the ritual at least once per week until the mixture is gone.

Truthful Trinket Charm to Expose the Facts

Remember that time you had a hunch that some details were missing from someone's story, and you were right? When you feel something is off, etch the words "To reveal the Truth" into a purple candle. Light it, then take a trinket, a piece of jewelry, or a sodalite stone and pass it safely above the candle flame. As you do this, focus on the situation and the facts that need to come to light. Let the candle burn out, or respectfully extinguish it and relight it consecutively with the same intention until it has burned all the way down. Wear or carry the item with you, then ask the person in question about the situation.

Self-Reflection Charm for Unhelpful Behaviors

When you notice behaviors of yours that aren't particularly helpful in your relationships, use this simple working to capture and release them. During a full moon, lock a mirror by drawing an "X" across it with anointing liquid using your finger. Bring the mirror outside under the moonlight and gaze at yourself for a moment. Contemplate the behaviors that you want to release. Leave the mirror out so that the moon can cleanse the mirror and your behaviors, then bring it back inside in the morning. Before putting the mirror away, gaze upon your new self.

KINDRED SPIRITS CALL TO ATTRACT NEW FRIENDS

They say carrying a passionflower will attract friends. Well, when you're done with this spell, you're going to be popular! It amps up passionflower's power with color and sigil magick. Performing this ritual on a Sunday helps fire up the action of a customized sigil you'll create for your particular intentions. And the element of air carries your message, ensuring that companions far and wide will hear your call.

Materials

Yellow candle

Sewing pin or something else sharp for etching

Dried passionflower

⤛⤜ Instructions ⤛⤜

1. On a Sunday, etch a custom sigil designed for your intention (e.g., to attract like-minded friends) into the candle three times, stacked on top of each other from top to bottom.

2. Place the candle in your window, light it, and focus your intention on feelings of warmth and friendship as you watch the flame glow bright.

3. Let the candle burn until it just burns through the first sigil you etched. Then respectfully extinguish the flame and sprinkle the dried passionflower in the window around the candle.

4. On Monday, light the candle again and focus your energy on attracting warm, supportive friendships. Once the candle has burned through the second sigil, respectfully extinguish it.

5. On Tuesday, light the candle again, allowing it to burn through the third and last sigil.

6. Gather the passionflower from your windowsill, take it outside, and say:

   "I beckon to you my kindred spirit,

   beneath the silence, you can hear it.

   Before my eyes, you shall appear;

   this witch's call is crystal clear."

7. Blow the passionflower into the air.

RITUAL FOR STRENGTHENING GOOD RELATIONSHIPS

Think of these little container charms as magickal friendship bracelets—you'll make one for you and one for someone special. Oak trees, known for their super-tough wood, represent strength, endurance, and longevity. Agate brings you balance and harmony, while garnet strengthens friendship and trust. You'll seal everything in with red wax to symbolize power and determination. This working calls on the Universe, but feel free to call on any spirit you resonate with instead. And if you prefer to have something to carry with you, you can use bottle pendants or keychain containers.

Materials

2 small bottles with corks

Salt

Blue agate and garnet chips

Oak leaves

Red candle or sealing wax

ᖆᖆᖆ Instructions ᖆᖆᖆ

1. Add a layer of salt to your cleansed bottles and say:

   "I bless and protect the bond that we share."

2. Add the garnet chips in a layer, then say:

   "I call to the Universe to hear my prayer."

3. Add a layer of blue agate chips and say:

   "No river wide, no mountain high."

4. Add a layer of oak leaves, then say:

   "No holler low beneath the sky."

5. Cork the bottles, then seal them by dripping red candle wax or sealing wax over the top. Finally, say:

   "Our bond is blessed, never unbroken.

   This is my intention, as it is spoken."

6. Keep one bottle for yourself and give the other bottle to the person with whom you want to strengthen your relationship.

DRINK OF SACRED UNITY TO BLESS A COMMITMENT

This elixir can bolster any type of partnership, be it romantic or friendly, but it's perfect for blessing a commitment made by two individuals. You can prepare it with either Riesling or white grape juice—infusing the liquid with the essence of abundant love is what matters most. Cardamom and vanilla are key ingredients, each imbued with pure love and desire, while honey sweetens and strengthens the union, making it stick.

Materials

1 (750-milliliter) bottle Riesling
or white grape juice

½ gallon mason jar with noncorrosive lid

4 or 5 cardamom pods

1 or 2 vanilla beans or 1–2 teaspoons
pure vanilla extract

½ cup honey

Instructions

1. Pour the wine or juice into the jar.

2. Lightly crush the cardamom pods, then add them to the jar. Split and scrape the vanilla beans, and add the beans and their contents (or the vanilla extract) and honey to the jar. Stir gently to combine.

3. Secure the lid and let the mixture infuse in the refrigerator for 5 to 7 days. Be sure to shake your intention into the jar a few times. You can also taste the infusion periodically and adjust the infusion time based on your preference for flavor intensity.

4. Once the infusion reaches your desired flavor, strain the wine to remove the spices and transfer it back to the original wine bottle or another clean beverage container to chill in the refrigerator.

5. Serve your cardamom and vanilla–infused wine to all who wish to bless the commitment.

LAVENDER ROSE WHISPER BALM FOR IMPROVED COMMUNICATION

Not only is this the best balm for dry lips and skin, it's also crafted to keep you from putting your foot in your mouth. Thanks to rose, lavender, and a bit of honey to sweeten the things you say, you'll communicate with only love when you wear it. Create a double boiler by placing a smaller heatproof bowl inside a larger pot filled with 1 to 2 inches of water. Then simply heat and incorporate your ingredients in the smaller bowl as the outer water slowly melts them.

Materials

2 tablespoons beeswax pellets, calendula pellets, or grated beeswax

2 tablespoons coconut oil

2 tablespoons shea butter

1 teaspoon honey

1 teaspoon jojoba oil

5 drops lavender essential oil

5 drops rose essential oil

3–5 empty lip balm tubes or tins

Small funnel

Instructions

1. To a double boiler set to low, add the wax, coconut oil, shea butter, and honey.

2. Let the mixture melt and blend as you hold your hands over it and say:

   "From the mind, through the lips,

   this is where communication sits.

   To only speak clearly and sweet,

   I call transparency to me."

3. After the mixture is completely melted, remove it from the heat and stir in the jojoba oil and essential oils.

4. Using the small funnel, pour the mixture into the lip balm tubes or tins and allow it to solidify.

STILL WATERS SPELL
TO STOP GOSSIP

There's no gossip like small-town gossip. Everyone's a familiar face, and you can bet they've heard something about you. And what are offices—both physical and virtual—if not small towns of their own? Regardless of where it happens, if someone is gossiping about you, this spell can help freeze their chattering teeth (metaphorically speaking). Feverfew offers protection, clove is the go-to for banishing gossip, the number nine symbolizes endings and beginnings, and lemon destroys any ill will sent your way.

Materials

Dried feverfew

Salt

Freezer-safe container with lid

Pen and paper

Water

Fresh lemon

9 cloves

Instructions

1. Add the feverfew and salt to the container.

2. Write on the paper the name of the person who is gossiping about you. If you don't know who that person is, then write "Slanderous being."

3. Place the paper in the container and fill it with water.

4. Slice the lemon into wheels so you have enough to cover the surface of the water in the container.

5. Press the cloves into the lemon wheels, then place them in the container so they cover and seal the contents inside.

6. Secure the lid and put the container in the freezer. Keep it there until the gossip stops. Then throw the contents into an outdoor trash bin.

LOYAL LOVER'S SPELL
FOR FIDELITY & TRUTH

Protect the connection you share with your romantic partner when you cast this spell that intertwines devotion and honesty. Sodalite ensures that truth shall flow freely. Elder, a revered and sacred tree, shields your love, while skullcap provides emotional harmony. Using personal-tie items will tether your partner's energy to yours, ensuring they remain captivated by your unique qualities.

Materials

Pouch or cloth and string

Dried cardamom, elderflower or elderberry, skullcap, and sunflower

Selenite (or satin spar) and sodalite stones

Strand of your hair

Strand of your partner's hair or other personal-tie item

Instructions

1. Add the sunflower, cardamom, elder, skullcap, sodalite, and selenite (or satin spar) to the pouch or cloth.

2. Place your strand of hair in the bag with your partner's personal-tie item while saying:

    "Magick within,

    seeking truth,

    a bond between me and you.

    There's no one else,

    of this, I'm sure.

    Passionate fidelity,

    our intentions are pure."

3. Hang the pouch over the doorway that your partner uses most.

GROWTH THROUGH GOODBYES
RITUAL FOR RELEASING THE PAST

When the moon is full, it offers a moment to look back at what we've achieved and how we got there—a time for gratitude and reflection on things that did not serve us in this cycle. In Tarot, the Death card is the card of endings, while The Fool card starts things anew. To encourage a fresh start, you'll combine both with water and basil for cleansing and chamomile for balance. Keep in mind that you'll need a way to both discard and refill the water. When you are done, you can drink the chamomile-infused moon water or use it to cleanse yourself.

Materials

Deep bowl

Water and access to sink/faucet

Death Tarot card

Dried basil

The Fool Tarot card

Dried chamomile

Jar or bottle

⇢⟩⟩⟩ *Instructions* ⟨⟨⟨⇠

1. On the night of a full moon, fill the bowl with water, then set it before you on top of the Death card. (It's better to do this under the full moon, but, if necessary, you can do it indoors.)

2. Gaze at your reflection in the water, as if staring at a mirror, and say:

   "Here I am, releasing ties

   from my past,

   I say goodbye."

3. Add the basil to the water and stir it three times counterclockwise.

4. Wash your hands, face, and feet with the water, focusing on releasing and cleansing while expressing gratitude for the lessons you've learned along the way.

5. Pour out the water, either outside or down the drain.

6. Refill the bowl with water and return to same spot. This time, set the bowl before you on top of The Fool card.

7. Look at your reflection again in the bowl of water. Study this person who is ready to leap into a fresh new start.

8. Add the chamomile to the water and stir it three times clockwise.

9. Say:

   "Here I am, a journey to start,

   with an open mind and renewed heart.

   Embrace the change, this transformation is true.

   I now step forth, a self anew."

10. Cover the water and let it charge under the moon and infuse with the chamomile for a few minutes or as long as overnight.

11. Strain the water into a lidded jar and keep it refrigerated for up to 2 weeks.

TRUE LOVE BLOOMS TEA TO TRANSMUTE WOUNDS INTO AFFECTION

Color magick and natural magick come together in this transformative tea blend, which aids in healing the wounds we've all encountered in relationships. Blue is a universal color of healing; pink is the universal color of love. And thanks to anthocyanins found in the blue butterfly pea flower, this tea's deep blue color changes to a vibrant fuchsia when you add a squeeze of orange. Elderflower, rose, and jasmine offer love and protection while enhancing spiritual connections, and calendula encourages passion. This mixture makes two cups of tea—perfect for sharing and mending a rift between two people.

Materials

2 cups water

1 teaspoon dried blue butterfly pea flower

1 teaspoon dried calendula

1 teaspoon dried elderflower

1 teaspoon dried jasmine

1 teaspoon dried rose

2 orange wedges

Teaspoon

⇥ Instructions ⇤

1. Boil two cups of water.

2. To a teapot or two tea infusers, add the blue butterfly pea flower, calendula, elderflower, jasmine, and rose.

3. Pour the hot water over the tea blend. Cover and let it steep for 5 to 7 minutes.

4. After steeping, strain the water or remove the infusers and pour the tea into two cups. Garnish each with an orange wedge.

5. Sit down in a quiet space and gaze into the deep blue tea, thinking about healing any wounds that you may carry from previous relationships, any shadows that may be blocking you from receiving true love, or any rifts between yourself and another.

6. When you are ready, squeeze the juice from the orange wedge into the cup and watch it transform from deep blue to a vibrant fuchsia.

7. Using the spoon, stir a heart into your cup of tea followed by six clockwise circles.

8. Enjoy your tea while concentrating on warmth and love.

EMOTIONAL HEALING THROUGH HEARTACHE SPELL

If you find yourself ending a relationship or needing to mend post-breakup, turn to this healing spell. You'll light a blue candle for emotional recovery and a pink candle for self-love while using a river stone as a conduit between healing-water energy and grounding-earth energy. Burying the stone in the earth infuses your working with stable, long-term results.

Materials

Blue candle

Pink candle

Clear quartz stone

River stone

Tranquilitea (page 69) or other soothing tea

Instructions

1. Once your mind is calm, light both candles. Place the clear quartz between them and say:

   "I bring healing and calm,

   for my spirit to ease,

   in this moment of stress,

   for my heart to release."

2. Bring the river stone to your heart, letting it absorb your heartache, while you say:

   "Element of earth, heal my heart.

   Allow this pain to depart."

3. While the candles burn down, brew some Tranquilitea.

4. Sit quietly while sipping the tea and feeling whole, complete, nourished, and healed.

5. Once the candles have burned down, bury the stone in the earth, preferably somewhere far away from you.

LIFE-FORCE REKINDLING RITUAL TO CALL BACK YOUR POWER

With this magick, you are bound to become the most empowered person in the room. Rose petals evoke a sense of calm and joy, while ginger and mustard aid in harnessing power, particularly at the end of a cycle or journey. The potent bay leaf will assist you in realizing your deepest desires. This working is best used after cutting someone or something out of your life.

Materials

Small bowl or plate

Salt

Fresh or dried rose petals

Ground ginger

Mustard seed

Permanent marker

Dried bay leaf

Red candle

Instructions

1. While channeling your focused intention on calling your power back, add the salt, rose petals, ginger, and mustard seeds to the bowl or plate.

2. Using the permanent marker, write on the bay leaf: "Calling back my power."

3. Place the candle in the center of the bowl or plate, light the candle, and watch it burn for a moment before saying:

   "I call back my divine essence.

   My life force is rekindling.

   I am stepping into my power."

4. Kiss the bay leaf three times, then crush it in your hands and sprinkle it around the candle. Let the candle burn all the way down.

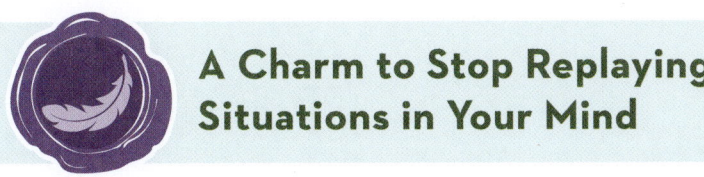

A Charm to Stop Replaying Situations in Your Mind

For those times when you seem to be stuck in a loop of winning arguments with yourself, try this charm to get some peace. Hold a white or yellow feather to your heart and say:

> "I release this situation and set it free.
> It will no longer plague me.
> My thoughts are free,
> and my mind is at liberty."

Blow the feather into the air and let it gracefully fall to the floor. Leave it there until the next day.

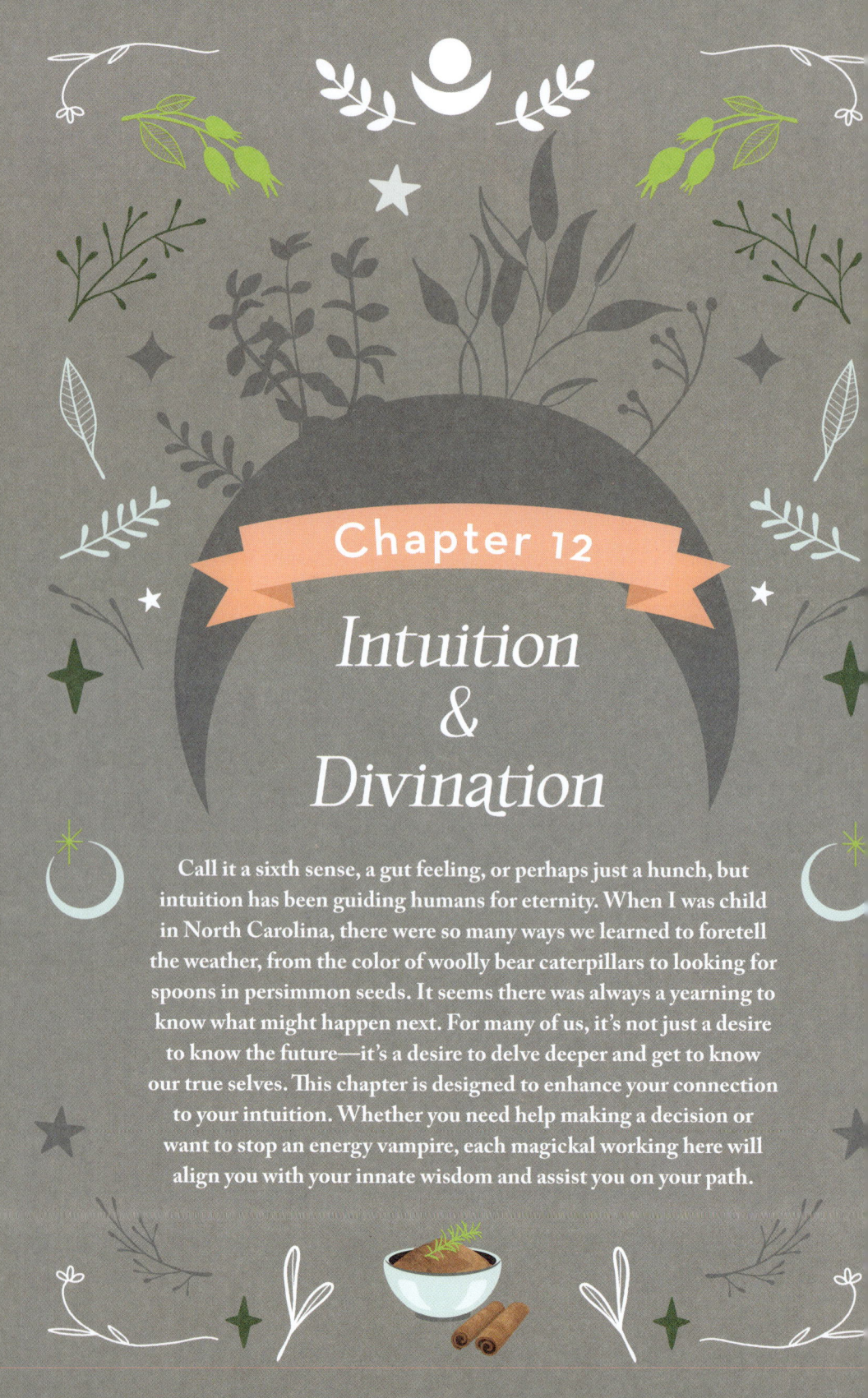

Chapter 12

Intuition
&
Divination

Call it a sixth sense, a gut feeling, or perhaps just a hunch, but intuition has been guiding humans for eternity. When I was child in North Carolina, there were so many ways we learned to foretell the weather, from the color of woolly bear caterpillars to looking for spoons in persimmon seeds. It seems there was always a yearning to know what might happen next. For many of us, it's not just a desire to know the future—it's a desire to delve deeper and get to know our true selves. This chapter is designed to enhance your connection to your intuition. Whether you need help making a decision or want to stop an energy vampire, each magickal working here will align you with your innate wisdom and assist you on your path.

BLESSED DRINK OF INNER KNOWING

A perfect blend of lemongrass and mint, this delicious drink enhances your psychic powers while promoting a sense of protection. Chamomile soothes your mind, making it easier to receive messages. This recipe yields about 16 ounces, but feel free to double it and add honey or another sweetener to taste, if desired. You can use moon-blessed ice cubes to enhance the spell; simply freeze Multipurpose Moonlight Cleansing & Blessing Essence (page 36).

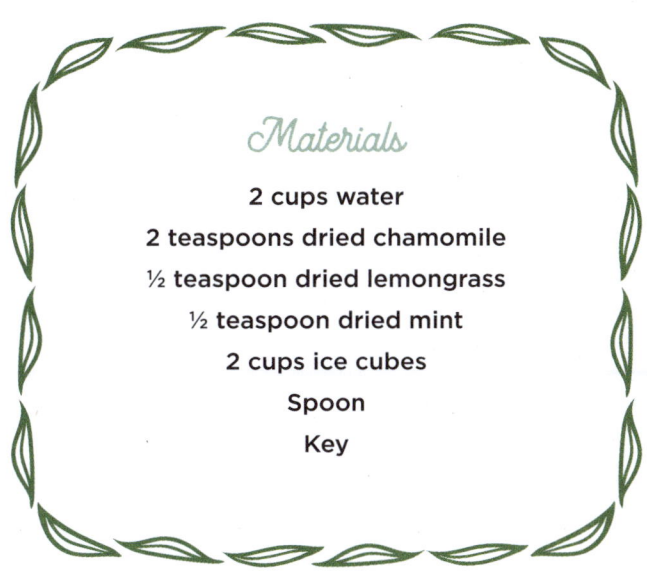

Materials

2 cups water

2 teaspoons dried chamomile

½ teaspoon dried lemongrass

½ teaspoon dried mint

2 cups ice cubes

Spoon

Key

1. Bring 2 cups of water to a boil. Turn off the heat, then add the dried chamomile, lemongrass, and mint.

2. Let the herbs steep for 5 minutes, then add 1 cup of ice cubes and stir them until they melt.

3. As you stir, move the spoon in a spiral and let your gaze soften on the mixture swirling in its container, letting your intention charge into the drink.

4. Once your mixture has cooled, strain and pour it into the glass over the remaining cup of ice.

5. Sip it while saying:

   "My mind and my heart are in sync

   with every sip I drink.

   I draw from the well of inner knowing;

   from within, my intuition is flowing."

6. When you have drunk all but the last sip, place the key in the glass and let it sit for a full day and night before drying it and discarding the last of the tea. Keep the key in a safe place, like on your altar.

7. When you seek inner knowledge, meditate or sleep with this key under your pillow.

Flip of Fate Coin Divination for Yes or No Answers

When I can't decide between two options, a coin flip never lets me down. I'm partial to pennies, but any coin with two distinct sides will do. First, designate one side for yes and the other for no. Then cleanse the coin by dropping it in salt water. Dry it and hold it loosely in both hands while contemplating the question. Next, shake it like dice while chanting: "With this flip, let fate be revealed." Toss the coin in the air and note which side it lands on for your answer.

SEER'S SERUM TO ENHANCE CLAIRVOYANCE

This serum is both easy to make and highly effective for those seeking the gift of foresight. Charging it with moonstone energy transforms it from a basic infused oil into a truly magickal elixir, enhanced by classic ingredients that promote intuition and metaphysical abilities. Apply a few drops of the serum between your brow and over your heart, or use it to anoint your divination tools.

Materials

Pint jar with lid

1 dried bay leaf

Dried lavender, mugwort, rosemary, sage, and wild lettuce

2 cinnamon sticks

Hempseed oil or grapeseed oil

Moonstone crystal

$\rightsquigarrow\!\!\!>$ *Instructions* $\ll\!\!\!\leftsquigarrow$

1. Add the bay leaf, lavender, mugwort, rosemary, sage, and wild lettuce to the jar. Be sure to pack it in well and fill the jar as full as you can, leaving only a small amount of space at the top.

2. Fill the jar with hempseed or grapeseed oil so that it completely covers the herbs.

3. Use one cinnamon stick to draw an eye in the center of the mixture before dropping it into the jar.

4. Use the second cinnamon stick to draw a triangle around the eye before dropping it inside the jar.

5. Drop the moonstone inside the jar, then secure the lid.

6. Hold your hands over the jar to charge it with your energy and focused intention while saying:

   "Sight beyond sight,

   visions I invite.

   The pathways are now open;

   clairvoyance has been woken."

7. Let the mixture infuse in a cool place away from direct light for 2 to 4 weeks.

8. When you feel it's finished, strain and discard the solids. Store the remaining serum out of direct sunlight.

INCENSE TO ENHANCE INTUITIVE & PSYCHIC ABILITIES

You can cast this spell any time you wish to boost your abilities, but it is especially beneficial when performed just before divination. Its purpose is to synchronize your personal energy with that of your divination tools or the energies around you. Star anise and true anise have a rich historical association with enhancing intuition. Clary sage and juniper, on the other hand, are known for providing clarity. When you blend these ingredients to create and use this incense, you harness the power of all four elements.

Materials

Mortar and pestle or electric coffee grinder

Dried star anise

Dried clary sage (or 10 drops clary sage essential oil)

Dried juniper (or 7 drops juniper essential oil)

5 dried bay leaves

Powdered pine gum

1 tablespoon makko powder

Small cup or bowl of water

·꓿꙰꓿· *Instructions* ·꓿꙰꓿·

1. With a mortar and pestle or electric coffee grinder, blend together the herbs (and oils, if using) and pine gum until you have a finely ground powder equaling about ½ cup.

2. Mix makko powder and a few drops of water into the herb mixture to form a paste. Shape the paste into incense cones or sticks and allow them to dry completely.

3. Light the dried incense, then pass your hands through the smoke as if washing them.

4. Use your hands to direct the smoke over your head, eyes, ears, mouth, and, finally, body, bathing it in an intuitive essence.

5. If you are using any divination tools, pass them through the smoke to cleanse them, bless them, and attune their energy with your own.

6. Allow the incense to burn completely into ash. Dip your finger in the small cup of water, then in the ash, and use it to draw a spiral over your heart before beginning your divination.

SPELL TO QUIET THE MIND OF INSECURITY

Mental chatter can be very distracting, especially when it's playing on your own insecurities. In this spell, you'll call upon the courage and love of yarrow when you are distracted by self-doubt. Selenite or satin spar lends clarity and mental focus while connecting you to a divine essence.

Materials

Fresh or dried yarrow

White pouch or sachet

Selenite or satin spar stone

Instructions

1. Place the yarrow and selenite or satin spar in the white pouch while saying:

    "Yarrow, yarrow, set me free.

    Now you've put my mind at ease."

2. Carry the bag with you. Anytime your mind begins to chatter, give the bag a squeeze and let the smell of the yarrow quiet it.

Witch's Prophesy Pillow for Dream Work

A dream pillow is a small pillow placed under a person's head while sleeping or over a person's eyes during meditation. Dream pillows are typically filled with fragrant herbs and flowers that correspond with sleep, dreams, or warding off nightmares. To make your own, choose two rectangular pieces of fabric, about 5 × 7 inches each, with a tight weave that are soft yet sturdy, like cotton or satin. Put them together, right sides facing each other, and sew along the edge, leaving a 3-inch opening at one end. Pull the fabric right side out, then use a funnel to fill the pillow with a few tablespoons each of rice, dried chamomile, dried lavender, and dried mugwort. Then sew the opening shut.

Trust Dust to Align with Your Innate Wisdom

Anytime you feel disconnected from your inner knowing, whip up a batch of this powder to sprinkle intuition everywhere you go. Blend dried lavender, marshmallow, and rosemary into a fine powder. Pour it into a jar and set it outside during a full moon to charge and fuel its energy. Use this mixture to dress candles, in container spells, or to scatter along your path and illuminate your way.

ROSEMARY WREATH FOR DREAM RECALL

The fragrance of fresh rosemary is nothing short of magickal, but it can also enhance intuition and dream recall when used in this customizable wreath. Incorporating an image of The High Priestess Tarot card gives it a boost, but you can use a hand-drawn crescent moon if you don't have a Tarot deck. You can also add other plants and crystals of your choosing to amplify a particular goal. Repeat this working monthly for continuous benefits.

Materials

10 sprigs fresh rosemary

Floral wire

Purple cord or embroidery floss

Decorations matching your intention (optional)

The High Priestess Tarot card

Instructions

1. Use the fresh rosemary to create a small circular wreath by attaching the sprigs to each other, end to end, with floral wire.

2. Wrap the purple cord or embroidery floss around the wreath, leaving wide gaps.

3. Tie off the cord, then begin wrapping a piece of floss in the opposite direction to make a crisscross pattern. Once you are happy with the look of it, tie it off. If you'd like to add additional decorations, do so now.

4. Position the wreath over The High Priestess card, which should sit in the center.

5. Holding your hands above the wreath, charge it with your energy and communicate your focused intention to have the rosemary aid you.

6. When you feel ready, hang the wreath over your bed. Keep it there for about a month, at which time you can deconstruct it and save the dried rosemary for other workings, such as Trust Dust (opposite).

ASTRAL INSIGHT SPELL FOR ENHANCED LUCID DREAMING

This simple sachet delivers powerful results when placed under your pillow to provide insights from intuitive and lucid dreams. Caraway and comfrey offer protection during your astral travels, bistort strengthens your connection with intuition, lemongrass enhances your perception of otherworldly realms. A broom adds another layer of protection for productive dreams.

Materials

Pouch or sachet

Poppy seeds

Dried bistort, caraway (or caraway seeds), comfrey, and lemongrass

1 dried bay leaf

Moonstone crystal

Broom

Instructions

1. Fill the pouch with poppy seeds, caraway, bistort, comfrey, lemongrass, and the bay leaf.

2. Focus on your intention and call upon corresponding energies by saying:

   "Caraway for mental agility,

   bistort for psychic powers,

   lemongrass for intuitive ability,

   comfrey for safety during astral travels."

3. Kiss the moonstone and hold it between your brows for a time that feels right before adding it to the pouch and drawing it closed.

4. Place the pouch under your pillow and the broom under your bed before going to sleep for the night.

BREW OF INSIGHT BAY LAUREL TEA READING

My first experience with tea-leaf reading was not with tea at all but with Turkish coffee. A friend made it for me and served it in small, elaborately decorated cups. Beneath them sat delicate saucers which, I would later learn, had an important role to play. As we sat together at my kitchen table one chilly afternoon, cold hands clutched around tiny, hot cups of coffee, I learned the art of tasseography. This is a form of divination that involves interpreting the patterns and symbols formed by tea leaves or coffee grounds at the bottom of a cup.

For this ritual, we'll be using bay leaves, which have a long history in divination. If you don't have a teacup and saucer, a mug and small plate work just as well. When interpreting the leaves, pay attention to the position of the symbols. Symbols closer to the top of the cup may indicate events in the near future, while those at the bottom may relate to the distant future. A symbol close to you may indicate something personal, while something farther away may mean a distant energy. A straight line might suggest a smooth journey, whereas a wavy or broken line could signify obstacles or changes. And symbols that are close together may suggest a combination of energy or events.

Materials

Water

1 cinnamon stick

Teacup and saucer

1 sprig fresh rosemary

3 dried bay leaves

<h2 style="text-align:center">⇢⇢⇢ Instructions ⇠⇠⇠</h2>

1. Boil water for the tea.

2. Use the cinnamon stick to cleanse your cup and saucer by running it counterclockwise three times around the top and inside of the cup and over the plate.

3. Place the cinnamon stick and sprig of rosemary inside the cup.

4. Crumble the bay leaves in your left hand while thinking of your question, then drop them into the cup.

5. Pour the hot water over the herbs in a clockwise direction, filling the cup, and let the brew steep for 5 minutes.

6. Stir the brew clockwise while thinking of your question, then remove any large bay-leaf pieces floating on the top. Set them aside.

7. Sip the tea in a focused, meditative state, leaving a small amount of liquid behind and allowing the bay-leaf remnants to gather at the bottom of the cup.

8. Holding the cup in your nondominant hand, give it a gentle clockwise swirl to move the bay-leaf remnants.

9. Quickly turn the cup over onto a saucer or plate, allowing any remaining liquid to drip out onto the saucer. Interpret the patterns and shapes left behind in the teacup by the bay-leaf remnants. Here are a few possible symbols to look for and their interpretations, though there are many in-depth descriptions available if you want to be more thorough.

   Anchor: Stability and security

   Bird: Good news or messages

   Cross: Challenge or obstacle

   Whole circle: Unity or completion

   Incomplete circle: Something left unfinished

   Heart: Love and affection

   Tree: Growth and prosperity

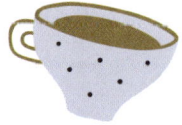

Ancient Bay-Leaf Divination

Rooted in ancient Greece and Rome, the leaves of the bay laurel tree held many important roles. As these leaves are sacred to the god Apollo, they were often used to make wreaths and crowns for poets, athletes, and victors in various contests. The Pythia at the Oracle of Delphi used them to relay divine messages. Some suspect that they used the toxic bitter bay (Nerium oleander), commonly known as oleander, but we'll be sticking to sweet bay (Laurus nobilis).

The most common way to use bay leaves for divination involves burning the leaf in a candle flame, fire, or another heat source, and then interpreting symbols, images, or signs in the leaf's curling, smoking, and burning. This can be especially helpful when you've written your manifestations or wishes on a bay leaf. If it sparks and burns fast, your goal has extra energetic support. If the leaf slowly smolders or does not burn well, your goal lacks energy. This is a good indication that you should do more to charge and fuel your intention (see Energize Your Spells: Fueling Your Magick on page 147).

You can also discover if you have a strong connection to your intuition by touching a bay leaf to your forehead and then burning the leaf. A vibrant flame means a strong connection, whereas a weak or flickering flame may suggest the need for more focus or inner work. And if you're seeking to deepen your spiritual connection, burn a bay leaf and pay attention to the smoke patterns. A steady, upward-rising smoke means a clear connection to higher realms. A smoke-free smolder can mean that you need to put more effort into communing with them.

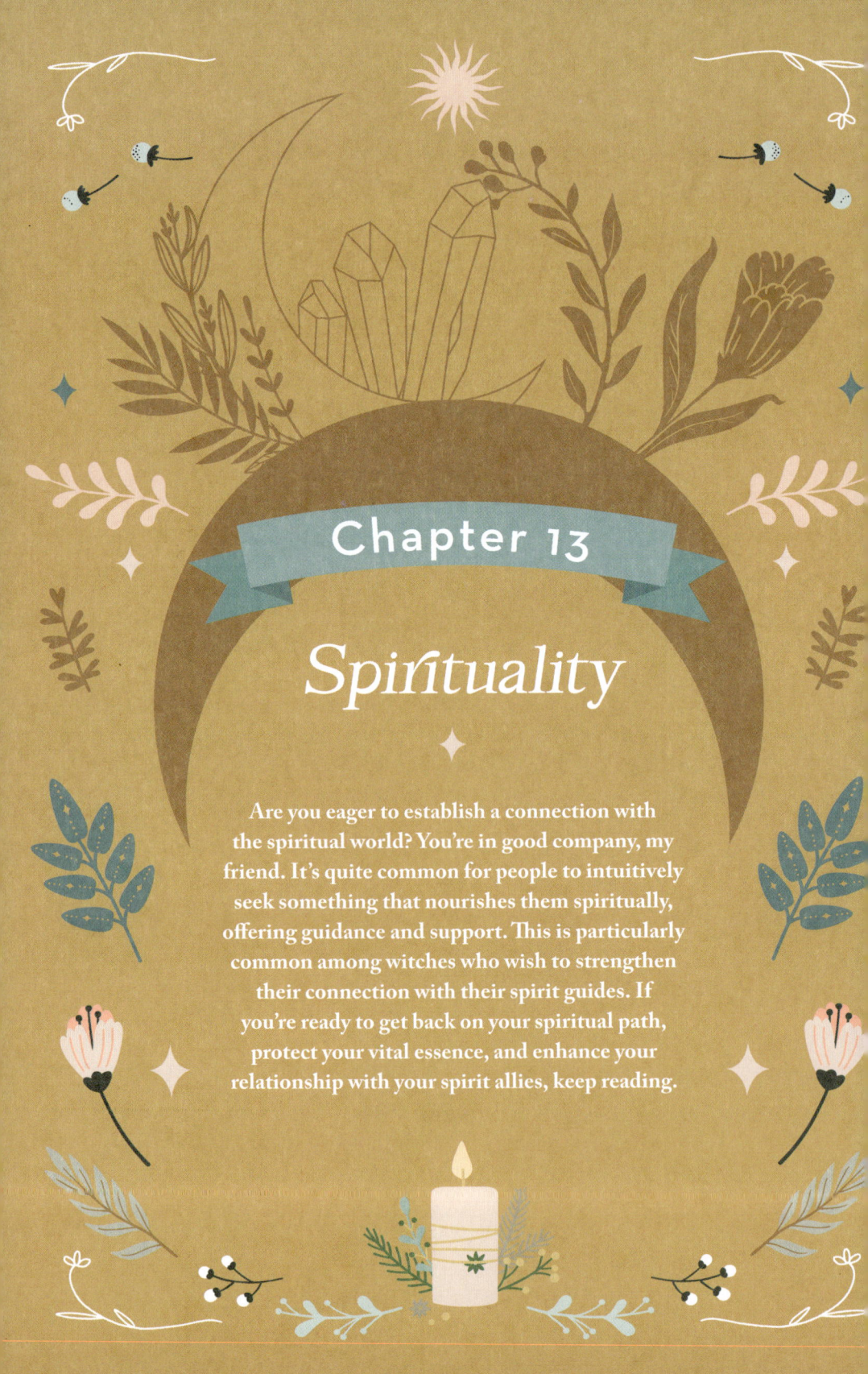

Chapter 13

Spirituality

Are you eager to establish a connection with the spiritual world? You're in good company, my friend. It's quite common for people to intuitively seek something that nourishes them spiritually, offering guidance and support. This is particularly common among witches who wish to strengthen their connection with their spirit guides. If you're ready to get back on your spiritual path, protect your vital essence, and enhance your relationship with your spirit allies, keep reading.

SOUL REFLECTION FOR CALLING YOUR SPIRIT GUIDES

Spirit guides are nonphysical beings or energies that provide assistance, support, and protection. They can come in various forms, and each person likely has multiple spirit guides who support them. You can call upon your guides to help you in decision-making, for emotional healing, dream interpretation, divination, and more. Try combining this ritual with Incense to Enhance Intuitive & Psychic Abilities (page 189) to strengthen your energetic connection.

Materials

Altar decorations

White candle

Incense

Journal and pen

⇝⇛ *Instructions* ⇚⇜

1. Decorate your altar with items that evoke feelings of fulfillment, gratitude, and serenity. Place a white candle in the center and the incense nearby.

2. Light the incense and candle before closing your eyes.

3. Begin to focus on your breathing. Inhale deeply through your nose, counting to four, and then exhale slowly through your mouth, counting to four. Do this as many times as feels right.

4. Envision a serene beach at dawn, the waves rhythmically crashing with your breath, and the sunrise just approaching. See the sun peeking at you slowly in the distance before it begins to bathe you in its light. Picture the surroundings vividly, noticing the sights, sounds, smells, and sensations of the beach in the morning.

5. Now bring your focus to your inner light and call upon your spirit guides by saying:

   "I call upon my spirit guides and invite you to join me."

6. Once you feel a presence that is safe and familiar to you, ask questions and seek guidance. You may simply ask:

   "What message do you have for me?"

7. Allow yourself to listen and feel for any responses or feelings that arise, and be open to receiving insights, answers, or messages in whatever form they come. They may communicate through thoughts, feelings, images, or a sense of inner knowing.

8. When you feel ready, thank your spirit guides for their presence and guidance. Then slowly return your awareness back to the serenity of the beach. Feel the sand beneath you and hear the gentle rhythm of the waves aligning with your breath once more.

9. Wiggle your fingers and toes and open your eyes slowly to come back to the present moment.

10. Journal about your experience and note any insights or messages you received.

Meeting Your Guides for the First Time

If you're meeting any spiritual guide for the first time, take a moment to familiarize yourself with their appearance and energy. To confirm their identity, ask for a physical sign, like spotting three butterflies of a unique color or multiples of numbers. Another way is to ask for confirmation in a dream.

SPELL FOR GOING WITH THE FLOW

"Sometimes you've just got to go with the flow and not plan everything," my husband said, as I questioned him for the fifty-ninth time about our plans for the holiday break. What can I say? I'm a planner. But there comes a time in every witch's life when you've got to let go of expectations and attachments and let the Universe take the wheel. In times like these, I like to call upon the energy of water. After all, there's nothing quite as fluid.

Materials

Large glass of water

Small bowl

Salt

Dried borage

Instructions

1. Holding the large glass of water, speak to it, saying:

   "Water, gentle and free,

   may your fluid grace inspire me.

   A steady stream, wherever I go;

   as does water, like a river, I flow."

2. Pour some water from the glass into the empty bowl.

3. Add the salt and borage to the bowl.

4. Sip the remaining water from the glass as the bowl's water absorbs your focused intention.

5. After finishing the glass of water, use the water in the bowl to wash your hands, visualizing ties and attachments to specific outcomes flowing away and down the drain. Then pour out the remaining water.

KNOT & BROOM SPELL TO SAFEGUARD YOUR SPIRITUAL JOURNEY

Embarking on a spiritual journey can be quite an adventure. To safeguard this journey, craft this amulet bag for protection. Working with knots channels your magick, and incorporating the color purple enhances intuition. A trusty broom offers protection while flying through spiritual realms, and protective stones provide guidance as you explore the unknown. Just be sure to cleanse and charge the charm under the full moon regularly to maintain its effectiveness.

Materials

Purple cord or yarn, about 10 inches long

Miniature craft broom

Small pouch (big enough to hold the cord, broom, and crystals)

Moonstone, sodalite, and tiger's eye crystals

Instructions

1. As you tie three knots in the purple cord, say (one word per knot):

    "Safeguarding."

    "Insight."

    "Discernment."

2. Tie the knotted cord to the broom and place both in the pouch with the moonstone, sodalite, and tiger's eye.

3. Place the pouch under your pillow or hold it during meditation and spiritual rituals.

SPELL TO STOP AN ENERGY VAMPIRE

We've all experienced energy vampires—a.k.a. people or situations that can become incredibly draining on your life force. When you need a little energetic help to vanquish these not-so-mythical fiends, this spell is here to help. You'll create a protective barrier using willow and thorns from a prickly plant, as well as copper for warding off evil and salt for protection. For an added layer of security, consider using Raven Ward Multi-Use Protective Salt (page 51) and Botanical Shielding Oil (page 57).

Materials

Thorn or nail

Black candle

Anointing liquid

Small black box with lid

Salt

Black tourmaline stone

Dried agrimony, garlic, hyssop, and willow bark

Piece of copper

⇶ Instructions ⇷

1. During the waning moon, use the thorn or nail to etch the words "draining," "feeding," and "attacking" into the candle, starting at the bottom and moving toward the top.

2. Anoint the candle, moving away from you and being sure not to coat the wick. Then light the candle and place it to the side.

3. Fill the bottom of the small box with a layer of salt and place the black tourmaline in the center of it.

4. Add the agrimony, garlic, hyssop, and willow bark in a counterclockwise circle around the black tourmaline. After you do this, say:

   "With pure intent and will so strong,

   I stop you now and right this wrong.

   The boundary is set, the objectives are clear;

   I'm moving forward without fear.

   Go away now, you have no power here."

5. Close the box (tape or tie it shut, if needed) and seal it with wax drippings from the black candle.

6. Let the candle burn down, periodically dripping more wax over the box and paying special attention to the seams.

7. Anoint the copper and four corners of the box with your liquid, then place the box by your primary entrance with the copper on top.

8. On the next waning moon (in approximately 1 month), throw the box in an outside trash bin. Keep the copper with you as a protective amulet.

Copper as a Conductor of Energy

Copper has been used worldwide for its magickal properties, which include love, luck, protection, healing, spirituality, beauty, creativity, and attraction. The large number of free electrons in copper makes it an efficient conductor. In modern magickal practices, the most effective copper objects are jewelry, antique items, nuggets, shavings, or wire. You can use pennies, but keep in mind that they contain more zinc than copper.

SPIRITUAL RECONNECTION RITUAL TO GET BACK ON YOUR PATH

While I enjoy elaborate group rituals, I also cherish small personal rituals performed at home. As a crafty witch, I often create garlands for protection and blessings in my practice. This particular one is handy for seeking assistance in reconnecting to your spirituality or discovering your spiritual roots. You can hang these little bottles over beds, meditation altars, or sacred spaces or carry one with you for daily intuition. Elder, sacred in many traditions, offers you protection and wisdom, while mugwort brings out your true essence.

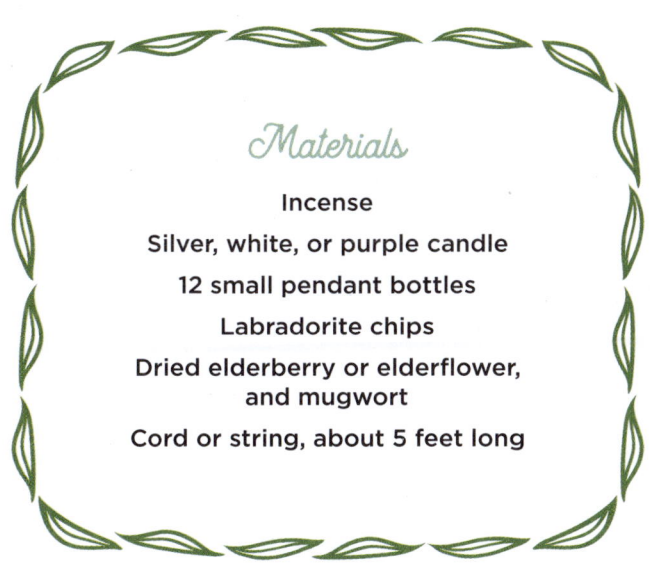

Materials

Incense

Silver, white, or purple candle

12 small pendant bottles

Labradorite chips

Dried elderberry or elderflower, and mugwort

Cord or string, about 5 feet long

⇢⇢⇢ *Instructions* ⇠⇠⇠

1. On the night of a full moon, light the incense and candle.

2. Fill the small pendant bottles with the labradorite chips, elderberry, and mugwort. As you do this, focus on your intentions and, as you add each layer of ingredients, visualize yourself climbing a staircase that leads you to reconnection.

3. Say:

   "I remove spiritual neglect,

   to allow my body, mind, and spirit to reconnect."

4. Secure the cork and drip the candle's wax over it, sealing in your intention.

5. String one of the bottles onto the cord and tie a knot in the cord. String the next bottle onto the cord, tie a knot, and repeat this process until you've added all of the bottles to the cord to make a garland. As you tie the knots, say:

   "Spiritual connection is here;

   I now have the power to see.

   My vision is clear;

   my mind has been set free."

6. Let the candle burn all the way out or respectfully extinguish it and relight it consecutively with the same intention until it is finished.

7. Hang the garland over your bed, your altar, or another place where you tap into your spirituality.

Incense to Connect with Ancestors

In a mortar and pestle or an electric coffee grinder, combine dried patchouli, vervain, rue, sage, and yarrow; 6 threads of saffron; and 1 teaspoon of powdered pine gum until you have approximately ½ cup of ground mixture. To this, add 2½ tablespoons of makko powder and a few drops of water to create a workable paste. Shape the paste into incense cones or sticks and allow them to dry completely before burning. Burn this spirit-amplifying incense during meditation or magickal work when you want to connect with your ancestors.

SPIRITUAL ENERGY REJUVENATION RITUAL RINSE

We all have so much information coming at us from all places that it's overwhelming, to say the least. And that can have a big impact on your energetic connections. Give this ritual rinse a try when you need to refresh and rejuvenate your spiritual routine. You can use it as part of a larger ritual or as a mini magickal working within your everyday life. Rosemary offers protection, mint enhances psychic abilities, rose petals heighten insight, and nettle purifies.

Materials

1 quart water

¼ cup dried or 12 sprigs fresh rosemary

2 tablespoons dried or 6 sprigs fresh mint

2 tablespoons dried or ¼ cup fresh rose petals

2 tablespoons dried or ¼ cup fresh nettle

Quart jar with lid

Instructions

1. Bring the water to a roaring boil. Then reduce the heat to a low simmer and add your herbs.

2. As the herbs simmer, hold your hands safely over the mixture and charge it with your focused intention. Then use your hands to direct the steam over your head as you visualize it opening and releasing your energetic field, clearing away any stagnant energy that you may have picked up along the way.

3. Allow the mixture to simmer for about 30 minutes total. During this time, you can meditate and rest or do some other gentle activity.

4. Once the mixture is ready, carefully strain it into the jar and let it cool. Discard the herbs.

5. The next time you shower, use the water as a hair rinse after washing and conditioning. As you pour it over the crown of your head (with your head slightly tipped back so as not to get any near your eyes), feel it flowing down and away from you, cleansing any built-up, less-than-useful energy.

OIL OF AETHER TO COMMUNE WITH SPIRITS

This powerful blend is carefully crafted with ingredients to enhance spiritual practices. Usnea, also known as "old man's beard," symbolizes wisdom and longevity, and it's coupled with essential oils that are invigorating and inviting to spirits. You can apply this blend between the brows or on top of the head to amplify dream work and meditation experiences. It is also ideal for anointing yourself or your tools before divination rituals, and can be used on ancestor altars or during any work involving communication with spirits.

Materials

Pint jar with lid

Dried angelica root, mugwort, and usnea

Hemp seed oil

4 drops cypress essential oil

4 drops cedarwood essential oil

3 drops lavender essential oil

2 drops mastic essential oil

4 drops vetiver essential oil

Dropper bottles

Clear quartz chips

Instructions

1. Combine equal parts of dried angelica root, mugwort, and usnea to fill a clean pint jar while focusing on uniting the spirit, mental, and physical realms.

2. Add enough hemp seed oil to the jar to cover the herbs completely.

3. Secure the jar's lid and allow the mixture to infuse for 2 to 4 weeks in a cool, dark place, shaking your intention into it every few days.

4. After that time has passed, strain the mixture and discard the solids, but keep the oil in the jar. Then add the essential oils, secure the lid, and shake the jar with the intention of activating the magickal working.

5. Decant the oil into dropper bottles and add a clear quartz chip to each bottle to amplify the magick.

TAROT SPREAD FOR GUIDANCE ON YOUR SPIRITUAL GROWTH

In this Tarot spread, you'll utilize The High Priestess card to enhance your intuition while drawing an additional three cards. These three cards help determine the optimal path for your spiritual growth. The first card represents your current spiritual condition or where you are on your spiritual journey. It provides insights into your present mindset. The second card highlights any obstacles or challenges you're facing on your spiritual path. It can provide guidance on what you need to overcome or the shadows that you need to integrate. The third card offers guidance and insights on how to enhance your spiritual journey. It can suggest actions or perspectives that can help you grow spiritually. Bringing in the assistance of color magick with a purple, gray, or silver candle will enhance your divination. Fluorite offers mental balance, connection with intuition, and calming and stabilizing energy.

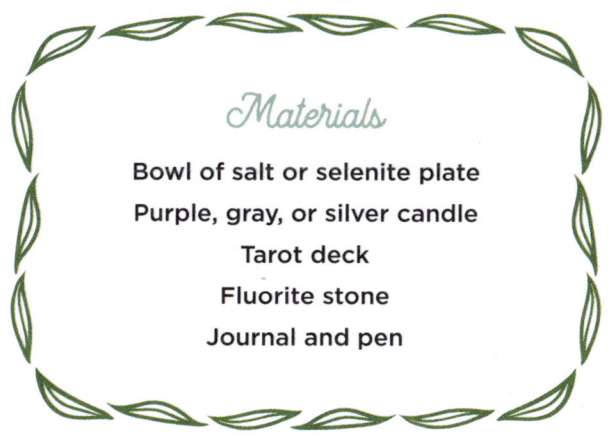

Materials

Bowl of salt or selenite plate

Purple, gray, or silver candle

Tarot deck

Fluorite stone

Journal and pen

✺ Instructions ✺

1. Place your deck on top of the salt or selenite to purify its energy.

2. Light the candle and spend some time meditating on your spiritual intentions and questions. Feel free to call your spirit guides to assist you.

3. When you feel ready, pick up your deck and find The High Priestess card, placing it at the top of your working space.

4. Place the fluorite crystal on top of The High Priestess card.

5. Shuffle the deck, then pull three cards.

6. Take your time to connect with your inner wisdom and interpret the cards. Trust your intuition. The first card signifies your current spiritual state, the second card represents your spiritual challenges, and the third card indicates your spiritual guidance. (If you're not familiar with Tarot, and your deck did not come with a booklet, you can turn to page 216 for simple interpretations.)

7. Write down your cards and the insights you gain from them to help you move forward on your spiritual path.

Correspondences & Substitutions

A great thing about natural magick is that every ingredient offers a bounty of beneficial properties that you can use for various purposes in your spellwork. So if you don't have a certain ingredient on hand, you can find several other items that will work well in its place. When seeking a substitution, consider the sympathetic properties of the ingredient. This involves thinking about what a particular plant or mineral is known for or associated with. For example, it's not surprising that rosebuds or rose petals are ideal for assisting with love spells, just like lavender seems like an obvious choice for sleep and peace. In this section, I have listed some of my favorite plants and minerals to mix and match, all organized by intention. Simply look up your need or desire to see the suggested substitutions.

Plants

Plants have a multitude of
magickal properties that align with their
sympathetic energy. When choosing a plant to work
with, consider the aspects that you most associate with that
plant. Allowing your intuition to inform you can go a long
way in choosing suitable substitutes or customizing spells.
Use the following list as a guide to help you
align your desires with similar energy.

Abundance and growth: Alfalfa, basil, honeysuckle, patchouli, sunflower

Ancestral work: Cedar, mugwort, rosemary, sage, yarrow

Banishing and breaking curses: Black pepper, cayenne pepper, garlic, rue, vervain

Communication and confidence: Bergamot, lemon balm, peppermint, sage, spearmint

Creativity: Basil, cinnamon, lemon verbena, orange, rosemary

Divination: Bay, jasmine, mugwort, rosemary, sage, tea, yarrow

Energy and vitality: Eucalyptus, ginger, ginseng, peppermint, rosemary

Fertility and sexuality: Damiana, maca, nettle, red raspberry leaf, yarrow

Grounding and stability: Cypress, mugwort, patchouli, vetiver

Harmony and peace: Chamomile, lavender, meadowsweet, passionflower, violet

Healing: Calendula, chamomile, comfrey, eucalyptus, plantain

Hex: Angelica, black salt, rosemary, rue, St. John's wort

Intuition and psychic development: Bay, clary sage, lemongrass, lemon verbena, mugwort

Love: Damiana, jasmine, lavender, patchouli, rose

Luck: Allspice, chamomile, clover, ginger, Irish moss, nutmeg

Money: Alfalfa, allspice, basil, chamomile, cinnamon, cloves, galangal, ginger, mint

Prosperity: Basil, bergamot, cinnamon, mint, patchouli

Protection from negativity: Black salt, black tourmaline, hyssop, juniper, rue

Protection: Angelica, basil, rosemary, rue, sage, St. John's wort

Psychic abilities: Bay, lemongrass, mugwort, yarrow

Purification: Cedar, frankincense, juniper, myrrh, rosemary, sage, sandalwood

Self-love and empowerment: Calendula, chamomile, jasmine, rose, rosemary

Sleep and dreams: Chamomile, hops, lavender, mugwort, valerian

Spirit communication: Frankincense, jasmine, lavender, mugwort.

Spiritual connection: Frankincense, myrrh, sandalwood, yarrow

Strength and courage: Carnation, dandelion, ginger, nettle, St. John's wort, thyme

A Note on Sourcing Ingredients

Ethical and sustainable sourcing of ingredients in magick involves respecting nature, supporting local communities, choosing fair-trade options, prioritizing eco-friendly practices, and practicing mindful consumption. Please be a responsible practitioner by honoring the environment and supporting fair practices.

Minerals

Like all of the ingredients used in a magickal working, minerals hold energetic components that can be leveraged in spells and rituals. Use the following list to find a mineral with the same vibrations as your needs and desires.

Abundance and growth: Citrine, green aventurine, moss agate, pyrite, tree agate

Ancestral work: Amethyst, Apache tears, black obsidian, clear quartz, selenite

Banishing and breaking curses: Black onyx, black tourmaline, obsidian, smoky quartz

Communication and confidence: Amazonite, blue calcite, blue lace agate, sodalite

Creativity: Carnelian, citrine, green jade, orange calcite, sunstone

Divination: Amethyst, blue kyanite, clear quartz, labradorite, lapis lazuli

Energy and vitality: Bloodstone, carnelian, red jasper, ruby, sunstone

Fertility and sexuality: Garnet, moonstone, rhodochrosite, rose quartz, ruby

Grounding: Black tourmaline, hematite, obsidian, red jasper, smoky quartz

Harmony: Amazonite, blue lace agate, green aventurine, rhodonite, rose quartz

Healing: Amazonite, amethyst, clear quartz, green jade, selenite

Hex breaking: Black tourmaline, jet, labradorite, obsidian, smoky quartz

Intuition: Amethyst, labradorite, lapis lazuli, moonstone, selenite

Love: Green aventurine, mangano calcite, rhodochrosite, rhodonite, rose quartz

Luck: Amazonite, citrine, green aventurine, jade, pyrite

Money: Citrine, garnet, green aventurine, moss agate, pyrite, tiger's eye, tree agate

Prosperity: Citrine, green jade, green moss agate, pyrite, tiger's eye

Protection: Amethyst, black onyx, black tourmaline, hematite, labradorite, obsidian, smoky quartz

Psychic abilities: Amethyst, azurite, fluorite, labradorite, lapis lazuli

Purification: Clear quartz, desert rose, labradorite, selenite, shungite

Self-love and empowerment: Garnet, prehnite, rhodonite, rose quartz

Sleep and dreams: Amethyst, blue lace agate, howlite, lepidolite, moonstone

Spirit communication: Amethyst, celestite, labradorite, selenite

Spiritual connection: Amethyst, apophyllite, celestite, clear quartz, selenite

Strength and courage: Carnelian, hematite, red jasper, sunstone, tiger's eye

Colors

Colors carry symbolic meanings throughout magickal traditions that align with specific energies and intentions. Next time you're working some magick, think a little deeper about ways to incorporate color magick correspondence, which can amplify your desired outcome. You can utilize colors through items like papers, inks, candles, ribbons, cords, plates, bowls, fabric, and more.

Black: Banishing, endings, protection, removing, repealing

Blue: Balance, element of water, healing, rest, tranquility, trust, wisdom

Brown: Grounding, prosperity, stability, well-being

Gray: Balance, neutralizing energy, peace, psychic abilities, shielding

Gold: Action, God, intellect, luck, riches, success, sun, wealth

Green: Element of earth, fertility, money, prosperity, stability

Orange: Action, adaptability, creativity, encouragement, honor, joy, strength, success, truth, uplifting

Pink: Family, friendship, harmony, heart connections, honor, love, self-love

Purple: Ambition, dreams, guidance, intuition, power, psychic abilities, the Universe or Divine, wisdom

Red: Action, bravery, conquering fear, element of fire, enthusiasm, fertility, love, passion, romance

Silver: Dreams, emotions, goddess, inner work, intuition, lunar influence, transformation

White: All-purpose (it can substitute for any color), cleansing, serenity, spirituality

Yellow: Element of air, intelligence, intent, success, will

Tarot Cards

There are many ways to interpret Tarot cards, from utilizing guides (like the ones that come with most card decks) to studying the cards' numerology and imagery or accessing your intuition. When incorporating Tarot into spells and rituals, a simple interpretation will often do. Here is a fundamental explanation of what each card means.

Major Arcana

The Fool (0): New beginnings and spontaneity

The Magician (I): Manifestation and personal power

The High Priestess (II): Intuition and inner knowledge

The Empress (III): Nurturing and abundance

The Emperor (IV): Authority and structure

The Hierophant (V): Spiritual guidance and tradition

The Lovers (VI): Union and choices from the heart

The Chariot (VII): Triumph through determination

Strength (VIII): Inner strength and resilience

The Hermit (IX): Solitude and inner reflection

The Wheel of Fortune (X): Change and cycles

Justice (XI): Fairness and balance

The Hanged Man (XII): Surrender and letting go

Death (XIII): Transformation and new beginnings

Temperance (XIV): Harmony and balance

The Devil (XV): Temptation and materialism

The Tower (XVI): Sudden upheaval and revelation

The Star (XVII): Hope and inspiration

The Moon (XVIII): Intuition and subconscious

The Sun (XIX): Success and joy

Judgment (XX): Reckoning and rebirth

The World (XXI): Completion and fulfillment

Tarot Suits

Cups: Emotions and intuition

Pentacles: Money, material matters, stability, and health

Swords: Ideas, creativity, knowledge, and boundaries

Wands: Desires and passions

Numbered Cards

Ace (1): Inspiration, beginnings, and clarity

Two (2): Planning, connection, and decision-making

Three (3): Exploration, celebration, strategy, and success

Four (4): Celebration, introspection, contemplation, and stability

Five (5): Challenges and conflict

Six (6): Success, harmony, relief, and generosity

Seven (7): Reflection, choices, evaluation, and assessment

Eight (8): Progress, withdrawal, wisdom, and discipline

Nine (9): Attainment, reflection, and wisdom

Ten (10): Fulfillment, culmination, completion, and abundance

Court Cards

Pages: Messengers

Knights: Active pursuit

Queens: Expertise

Kings: Leadership

Index